DATE DUE

The Poet Swift

The University Press
of New England

Sponsoring Institutions
Brandeis University
Clark University
Dartmouth College
University of New Hampshire
University of Rhode Island
University of Vermont

The Poet Swift

Nora Crow Jaffe

The University Press of New England

Hanover, New Hampshire, 1977

The publication of this book was assisted by grants from the Hyder
Edward Rollins Fund of Harvard University and the Andrew W. Mellon
Foundation. Oxford University Press has given permission to reprint
300 lines of poetry from *The Poems of Jonathan Swift*, edited by
Harold Williams, 2nd edition, 1958.

For My Parents

Preface

With the shift in the critical estimation of Swift's poetry has come a strange moment of awkwardness. The subject is ripe for treatment, inviting to those on the alert for fresh aspects of major writers. The critical climate is benign. Yet between the recognition of Swift's importance as a poet and the full examination of his poetry, the critics have noticed a hiatus. In a fairly recent bibliographical guide to Swift, Ricardo Quintana cited only one book-length study of the poems and only one nonspecific essay ("A Modest Appraisal: Swift scholarship and criticism, 1945-65," in *Fair Liberty Was All His Cry: A Tercentenary Tribute to Jonathan Swift 1667-1745*, ed. A. Norman Jeffares, London, 1967, pp. 353-354). Also in 1967, Rachel Trickett noted that even the critics friendliest to Swift had hardly done more than assert the importance of his verse, and she speculated that Swift's unusual approach to poetry "inhibited" criticism by seeming to cast doubt on verse-making as a craft (*The Honest Muse: A Study in Augustan Verse*, Oxford, 1967, p. 121). Critics feel some shame, Trickett believes, at the discrepancy between Swift's poetry and their analyses: Swift clearly did not want to write the kind of poems that academic critics are used to handling. Trickett's hypothesis may go far toward explaining this moment of critical unease, though it probably attributes to critics a greater capacity for being intimidated than they in fact possess. On a closer view, Swift's poems and his attitude toward poetry are not at all unprofessional. The difficulty lies in finding the right words to describe a poetry that is superficially simple but at its best can be emotionally over-powering, a poetry essentially popular in style but as suitable for an audience composed of one intimate friend as for the readers of a nation.

Even before the tercentenary celebration, some masterful discussions of individual poems showed that critics were finding their way toward an understanding of the poetry. Charles Peake provided an impeccable critique of "A Satirical Elegy on the Death of a late Famous General" based on the idea that the poem has "great emotional power controlled by taut and precise lan-guage and by firm poetic organisation" ("Swift's 'Satirical Elegy on a Late Famous General,'" *Review of English Literature*, 3, 1962, 81). C. J. Horne explained the generic background and the specific origin of "The Beasts Confession to the Priest," which he regards as the finest of Swift's verse fables (" 'From a Fable form a Truth': A Consideration of the Fable in Swift's Poetry," in *Studies in the Eighteenth Century: Papers Presented at the David Nichol Smith Memorial Seminar, Canberra 1966*, ed. R. F. Brissen-den, Canberra, 1968, p. 194). In his monumental biography, Irvin Ehrenpreis attacked and subdued particular poems, like "Baucis and Philemon," with his customary courage.

Since 1967 studies of individual poems have appeared at more and more frequent intervals, displaying both acuity and confi-dence. Writing on "Stella's Birth-Day" (1726/7), John Irwin Fischer has given the poem its first close reading, emphasizing (more than I do) the Christian resolution of the Stoic argument ("The Uses of Virtue: Swift's Last Poem to Stella," in *Essays in Honor of Esmond Linworth Marilla*, ed. Thomas Austin Kirby and William John Olive, Baton Rouge, 1970, pp. 201–209). Turning, then, to a poem much discussed, he analyzed the relation between Swift's verses on his own death and the conventional Christian meditation ("How to Die: *Verses on the Death of Dr. Swift*," *Review of English Studies*, New Series 21, 1970, 422–441). Peter J. Schakel ably continued the historic argument by posing questions about the politics of the poem ("The Politics of Opposition in 'Verses on the Death of Dr. Swift,'" *Modern Language Quarterly*,

35, 1974, 246–256). More recently, he has examined Swift's allusions to Ovid and Virgil ("Swift's 'dapper Clerk' and the Matrix of Allusions in 'Cadenus and Vanessa,'" *Criticism*, 17, 1975, 246–261). The work of A. B. England, James L. Tyne, Carole Fabricant, and Robert Uphaus confirms the impression that scholars are doing more and better criticism of Swift's poetry than ever before. Yet no critic has come forward with a comprehensive study of the poems in general. Shorter studies of the poems by C. J. Rawson and the late W. K. Wimsatt are soon to be published. Their attention to the subject makes the lack of a longer overview especially pointed.

The readers of English literature have not waited for the critics to tell them why they like Swift's poetry. They have enjoyed and demanded from their anthologists such poems as "Mrs. Harris's Petition" and "Verses on the Death of Dr. Swift" as if Swift's importance as a poet were a fact confirmed since his time. In nineteenth-century popular anthologies, Swift is at least as well represented as Gay and Prior, and sometimes as well represented as Pope. *The Poets of Great Britain* (London, 1807) devotes two volumes to Swift, as does *The Works of the British Poets* (London, 1808). *The Works of the English Poets* (London, 1810) gives to Swift 170 pages, as compared with 300 to Pope and 150 to Prior. *The Works of the British Poets* (Philadelphia, 1819) contains one volume of Swift's poems, one volume of Gay's, and one and a half of Pope's. *The Book of Gems* (London, 1837) represents Swift as well as Gay, better than Prior, and slightly less well than Pope. *The Aldin Edition of the British Poets* (London, 1853) devotes as many volumes to Swift as to Pope. T. H. Ward, in *The English Poets* (London, 1881), chooses seven selections from Swift, thirteen from Pope, and four from Gay. Ernest Bernbaum uses two selections from Swift, nine from Pope, and none from Prior in his *English Poets of the Eighteenth Century* (New York, 1918). Twelve of Swift's poems appear in *An Anthology of Augustan Poetry* (London, 1931), and the same number of Pope's appear there. Swift is adequately, if not amply, represented in both *The Oxford Book of Eighteenth Century Verse* (1926) and *A Collection of English Poems 1660–1800* (New York, 1932). Perhaps the most heartening sign, after Swift's exclusion from *The Oxford Book of English Verse* (1900), is his appearance in *The New*

Oxford Book of English Verse (1972). Swift is, as he always was, a popular poet. This book is an attempt to provide a critical framework for the enthusiasm that his readers have felt all along.

Among those who enjoy Swift's poetry, I found many to help me in this enterprise. The late Reuben Brower read the manuscript with the greatest of care, suggesting revisions that made it consistently tighter and more to the point. John Kelleher gave me the benefit of his expert knowledge in matters of British history and culture. George Mayhew, a very generous man, allowed me to read the manuscript of his book on Swift's early life and art. His interest in the early stages of my work convinced me that a community of Swift scholars is not an impossible ideal. Bliss Carnochan first taught me to love Swift, leaving me with a debt more substantial than any number of acknowledgments could repay. Arthur Jaffe gave me criticism from a layman's point of view and helped to make the book more acceptable—in a way Swift would approve —to the "common reader." I am indebted to him for ferocious support. Frank Ellis, David Horne, Bill Oram, David Wise, Adele Glimm, and Thomas J. Crow contributed their knowledge of Swift, of eighteenth-century poetry, and of twentieth-century readers. I thank them all.

Cambridge, Massachusetts   N.C.J.
June 1977

Contents

The Poet Swift

1. Reading Swift's Poems

PERHAPS the major reason that critics have said so little about
Swift's poetry is that seemingly there is little to say. Anyone can
tell that a poem of Swift's is powerful or tender or vital or fierce,
but all the paraphernalia of New Criticism seems inadequate to explain why. Juxtaposing almost any passage from Pope with one
from Swift helps to make the problem clearer. Pope's verse, unlike
Swift's, is rich in the kind of allusion that invites us to pause and
contemplate worlds long past. In Book IV of *The Dunciad,* ll. 397–
436, he makes successive allusions to Milton, the Magi, his own
Iliad, Catullus, female slang, Spenser, the pastoral, and again
Milton—all without loss of grace, clarity, or significance. Removing
the allusions would diminish the passage: they provide the contexts in which it must be read.

Pope's verse is as rich in texture as in allusion. The closed
couplets and the end-stopped lines are additives that enforce a
faith in his powers of analysis. The prosody cooperates perfectly
with the argument. The medial caesuras reinforce the ironic con-
trasts. The weight the poet characteristically gives to individual
words makes reading his lines like turning a jewel to examine its
beauties:

Fair to no purpose, artful to no end,
Young without Lovers, old without a Friend,[1]

("Epistle to a Lady")

We begin with an ironic contrast between young and fair, on the one hand, and old and artful, on the other. It is a collective statement about how both kinds of women, though very different in some ways, lead miserable lives. As we read, however, the words re-adapt themselves in relation to one another, deepening the meaning of each successive half-line. The collective statement about young and old becomes an encapsulated biography, a sequential view of an archetypal woman. At the same time, we move from simple pity through stages of moral judgment to pity of a more complex kind. The state of being "Fair to no purpose" may be deplorable, but it is morally neutral. This beauty does not achieve the results appropriate to its value. Placement of the phrase "to no purpose" in the same position as the phrase "to no end" in the next half-line reminds us that the attainment of beauty may be a deliberate act in pursuit of a conscious goal. Insofar as it involves flattering poses, the posturing of models that Pope examines at large in this poem, it can be altogether as "artful" as anything old women might devise. Insofar as it involves cosmetics, it will remind us of all the Belindas who put on their armor at the dressing-table. The phrase "to no end" means more than its earlier analogue: it raises questions about motives, especially in light of the word "artful." What is the outcome of this art? As with Belinda, this kind of artist cultivates a resistance to sexual love as part of her attractiveness. The result, we might say more coldly than at first, is the state of being "Young without Lovers." The whole charade ends in old age without even a friend for comfort, much less a lover. The last half-line takes us back to pity, but with the clear-sighted realization that from youth to age, such a woman precipitates her own doom. The first, "collective," reading defines the misery common to womankind. The second, "sequential," reading explains how such misery comes to exist.

Pope's poetry provides an inexhaustible field for critical rumination. But without a new perspective and altered methods, the same scholarly intelligence that battens on Pope will starve on Swift, whose prosody rarely calls for analysis, whose argument seldom moves between and within half-lines, whose allusions seldom bring a whole literary world into being:

> But let me warn thee to believe
> A Truth for which thy Soul should grieve,
> That, should you live to see the Day
> When Stella's Locks must all be grey
>
> . . .
>
> Though you and all your senceless Tribe
> Could Art or Time or Nature bribe
> To make you look like Beauty's Queen
> And hold for ever at fifteen.[2]
>
> ("Stella's Birth-day. Written AD. 1720-21," 45-48, 51-54)

At the allusion to Venus, we do not stop to imagine the world of antiquity. No balance or antithesis, between or within the half-lines, calls our attention to parallel ideas. We do not find layers of meaning by rereading earlier lines in the light of later ones. Sweeping us along with the rhythm of the argument, Swift expects us to appreciate the implications of the poem as a whole, after one full reading. As a rule, the Swiftian couplet will not revolve slowly upon itself, elucidating ironies and fixing complex relationships between fictive worlds and contemporary life.

Some of Swift's poems, of course, are not so apparently artless as these lines from "Stella's Birth-day" (1720/1). We come to his poem "On Dreams. An Imitation of Petronius" (1724) with the reassuring sense that he could exploit prosody in familiar ways, along with the best of his contemporaries. In the verses "On Dreams" the form does imply the argument. The juxtaposed couplets in each four-line stanza assert a basic likeness between respectable and reprobated crimes:

> The drowsy Tyrant, by his Minions led,
> To regal Rage devotes some Patriot's Head.
> With equal Terrors, not with equal Guilt,
> The Murd'rer dreams of all the Blood he spilt.   (11-14)

The poet is equating the tyrant and the murderer by means of a formal, appositional structure. The method is much like Pope's in *The Rape of the Lock:*

Not louder Shrieks to pitying Heav'n are cast,
When Husbands or when Lap-dogs breathe their last,[3]

Swift is working in an atypical mode.

The first two lines of each of Swift's stanzas describe the dreams of men whose crimes the world exonerates, even exalts: the rabid tyrant, the pitiless soldier, the muckraking politician, the double-dealing lawyer, the deadly doctor, the negligent clergyman. The second two lines equate these men with those whom the world reviles: the murderer, the butcher, Tom-Turd-Man, the pickpocket, the hangman, the mounteback. At times, single phrases startle us with their possibilities, as when the poet says the murderer's guilt is "not equal" to the tyrant's. Is it more or less? Is Swift speaking of guilt as a private sense of wickedness, of guilt as determined by society, or of guilt as defined by ideal standards? The politician dreams of "Forfeitures by Treason got" (20). By the treason he falsely imputes to others? Or by the treason he commits himself in betraying the innocent? The clergyman is as much a quack as the mountebank, but he is not so clever. Perplexed by knotty points, he nods ambiguously over his text, while the sly mountebank receives the better pay.

The stanza comparing doctor and hangman yields only to the last stanza in its ingenuity. Assuming the prerogatives of God, the physician metes out life and death. Like God, he grants prayers, a husband's prayers for his wife's death. The only motive ascribed to him explicitly is the impulse toward acts of kindness—charity for long-suffering heirs. Without mentioning him at all, the second couplet of the same stanza reveals his true, mercenary motives:

The kind Physician grants the Husband's Prayers,
Or gives Relief to long-expecting Heirs.
The sleeping Hangman ties the fatal Noose,
Nor unsuccessful waits for dead Mens Shoes.   (27–30)

The last stanza of the poem seems at first to follow the same pattern as the previous six. The first two lines deprecate a kind of vice that society commonly tolerates. The senator and the guilty great take their places beside the tyrant, soldier, statesman, lawyer, doctor, and clergyman. The pattern now requires that the second couplet present a vulgar equivalent to this respectable vice, that it describe men universally despised. A poet less clever might have placed Walpole in the first couplet, but Walpole isn't even that respectable. His element is the mud of the last lines:

> The hireling Senator of modern Days,
> Bedaubs the guilty Great with nauseous Praise:
> And *Dick* the Scavenger with equal Grace,
> Flirts from his Cart the Mud in [Walpole]'s Face.   (35–38)

The line that ends the poem gets its ironic stateliness from an elegant distortion of syntax and a masterly handling of caesura. We pause briefly after "Cart," savoring the *r* and *l* and *i* and even expecting a bit of the beauty that usually succeeds a departure from prose syntax. The ensuing ugliness makes Walpole even dirtier than his presence in the wrong couplet would imply by itself. The technique of the last line is noticed because the poem as a whole calls for attention to such effects. Swift is working within poetic conventions instead of forgoing them.

The reader, who adjusts his expectations early in the reading, brings to each of the two kinds of poetry a different cast of mind. If a poem is formally spare, if its argument is not closely bound to its prosody, he will tend to read it in logical units, looking for a point of application. Rather than being caught up in a web of allusion, a literary world, he is likely to move out toward his own world. This degree of disengagement from the minutiae of the text may mean that he will read fast, paying scant attention to the secondary patterns of sound and rhythm. On the other hand, he will read a poem like "On Dreams" with a slow consideration that permits the appreciation of such effects. Poetic devices in the two kinds of poetry operate at different levels of consciousness. The reader almost never feels that Swift is doing clever things with caesuras—even when he is. One is often aware that Pope is executing brilliant maneuvers within a line or couplet and looks forward to the demonstration of poetic prowess that the poet leads him to expect. The subtle analysis of formal elements in a poem by Pope can therefore have all the emotional authority of "what oft was thought."

The attempt to treat a typical poem by Swift in the same way, as Maurice Johnson occasionally does, can be puckering as a persimmon: "Like phrases from Shakespearean song, the last couplet here combines rich sound and an impression of bright detail. The beat of 'hearD a suDDen Drum' is as capably handled as are the blunted vowels that follow in 'OR FOUND an EARwig in a PLUM.' These two unpretentious lines are hardly inferior to those by Herrick that Edith Sitwell singles out to praise for their beauty . . ."[4] All that Johnson says about *d's* and "blunted vowels" may be true, but one cannot help feeling that it is remote from the life of the poem.

Attempts to identify the origin of literary allusions in Swift can set off the same response. For the most part, what Roger Savage has said of "A Description of the Morning" (1709) is irrefutable. The argument takes its start from a proposition that we can readily accept: Swift is superimposing a picture of London life upon a picture of the classical *belle nature*.[5] As the essay expands to include Claude and Parnell and Bysshe and Caravaggio, however, the law of diminishing relevance goes into effect. One feels that the essay, propelled by its own method, is moving rapidly and un-controllably out of the orbit of the poem. Savage takes every parallel and develops it as fully as he can, and each is reasonably analogous to the poem. But in Swift's verse, more often than in Pope's, the pursuit of echoes can lead to a conclusion at odds with the primary meaning of a poem. Savage's conclusion—"Swift both chafes at the classical ideal because it seems so little relevant to the reality he sees in the Strand, and is drily ironic about the reality he sees in the Strand because it will not live up to the standards set by the classical ideal"[6]—is wrong insofar as it mini-mizes the importance of the crucial fact. Swift loves what he sees in the Strand.

Readers who listen to Swift's clues will pass lightly over matters of form and restrict any undisciplined tendency to let allusions burgeon. Significant areas of inquiry remain. In what follows I shall address such problems as the schools of poetry that might have influenced Swift in a broad sense; his original handling of methods he shares with many good poets—portraits, impersona-tions, the use of vivid and precise detail, the manipulation of figures from classical rhetoric; his attitude toward poetry, his ideas about good verse, and his motives in writing poems; and finally, in this chapter, his deployment of new rhetorical strategies and his projection of a fascinating personality to make his poems emphatically his own. One cannot analyze the poems formally, as verse technique, without a sense of monumental irrelevance.

This sense of irrelevance is not altogether related to the spareness of the poems. Swift's rhetorical strategy involves hiding his art, and the spareness itself is a consciously chosen style. Critical efforts at mining the poems reveal his technical virtuosity and prove that he could be attentive to verse technique even when his care would go largely unnoticed. Reacting against the devices of some of his predecessors, especially the love poets of the Renaissance and Restoration, he seems to induce in his readers an unwillingness to look at the formal elements of his poems by working openly against some poetic conventions, by declaring that he rejects poetic cant, and by presenting himself, in many of his poems, as a perfectly straightforward man, incapable of a poet's deviousness. The result of this concealment of poetic device is to focus attention on the subject matter and the poet's attitude. In directing attention away from the form and indicating the primacy of subject and attitude, Swift is putting into practice, in an exaggerated way, a tenet common in Augustan criticism.

Though he is not negligent about verse technique, it is not his particular area of expertise. The argument in many poems is only loosely related to the prosody, the allusions are usually restricted in their implications, and many of the images are not developed in especially interesting ways. Looking for formal density in Swift obscures his real merits. His poems create a density of another kind, making up in power what they lack in technical interest. "The Day of Judgement" (1731?), for example, initiates a subtle process of thought that takes place after, rather than during, the reading of the poem, at a time when the mind is more or less detached from the printed page. Valueing Swift for what he does best means appreciating his use of original rhetorical strategies and his skillful presentation of selected aspects of himself.

The writer of this kind of poetry runs some risks. Since the effect of formal spareness is to throw the emphasis partly on the mind of the poet, a failure in the process—a mistaken choice or a lapse of control—may result in our rejecting the poem and the man together. On the other hand, Swift's usual artistry in selecting the materials for each self-portrait from within himself and shaping them to achieve the desired response is a matter for critical judgment and praise, even though a particular poem may leave us feeling that we simply like Swift. As Maurice Johnson said in 1971, the "special quality" in these poems may be Swift's own "biographical presence."[7]

The reader of "Stella's Birth-Day. March 13. 1726/7" may like the poem because he likes the Swift he meets there. His response to the poem is especially dependent upon the poet because the verses are private and occasional, as well as spare in ornament and allusion. Swift is really not so much concerned to make a public case for virtue as to persuade Stella that virtue and happiness go hand in hand, that her goodness in life should make her death a little easier. Even the private case for virtue is subordinate to the communication of love. The poet is not so much concerned to persuade the dying Stella as to comfort her, without deviating from the truth, and to convince her of his affection. The argument operates on the reader by a process of identification. He puts himself in the position of either Swift or Stella, focusing on the two personalities in the poem. Swift's capacity for tenderness, his honesty, and his strength of mind are revealed for his appreciation. Sentimentality or bitterness on the poet's part would destroy the impression. The relationship between his artistic control and his "personal" control is particularly close. Swift must have attained a degree of distance from his feelings before he could begin to write, but the way the poem moves suggests that the writing itself helped make the feelings manageable.

The poet begins with a full concession to the seriousness of the situation. The phrase "whate'er the Fates decree" (1), like the later and similar "whatever Heav'n intends" (79), implies his willingness to face the bitterest fact that he and Stella can confront. The voice of a man able to see reality in the worst of lights predominates throughout the poem and confirms that the offered comfort is realistic. But in the first fourteen lines Swift is mostly occupied with a different stance toward his friend and toward his own feelings. Despite his recognition of her imminent death, he wants to postpone mourning and worry over her sickness and his old age and "mortifying Stuff" (8) about "Spectacles and Pills" (6). The homely images and the suggestion of a pun in "mortifying" establish a lightness of tone that belies the gravity in the first line and the rest of the poem. He does not want to talk about death. He wants to celebrate the day.

Yet the last of the prologue hints that his means of celebration will be more grave than "joyful" in the ordinary sense of the word, or at least that he will try to win cheer out of seriousness:

> From not the gravest of Divines,
> Accept for once some serious Lines. (13-14)

The earlier touches of humor have established his control and enabled him to fend off sentimentality, but this style has proved inadequate to the moment. The long central passage that follows (15-78) is not at all humorous, and the extended argument is clearly intended to comfort the two friends in the face of death. Swift has desired to put off the thought of death, but he has not done so. His honesty appeals to certain universal and unsophisticated emotions. His determination to argue stoically from "Reason" (9) and his recommendation of the stoic virtues of courage, contentment, and patience reinforce our admiration. As a clergyman, Swift could have turned to Christian doctrine to palliate the evils of death. Instead, he chooses to persuade Stella solely on rational grounds that virtue can make her happy and makes a temporary concession to atheism that Heaven and Hell might not exist as recompense for goodness and vice. The pain that goes into the effort to reason clearly, to work a consolation out of the most unpromising reality, communicates itself to us with great force. It is as central to the poem as the love that makes the consolation necessary.

In this middle section the love is only implicit, for Swift has suppressed everything personal. Abstract reasoning sets the tone. Stella herself becomes something of an abstraction, full of "Boldness" (43), "Courage" (45), "Detestation" (47), and "Patience" (49). Swift addresses her in the same words that an epic poet might use in speaking to his muse: "Say, *Stella*" (35). He distances her further by comparing her to the ultimate abstraction:

> (So Providence on Mortals waits,
> Preserving what it first creates) (41-42)

The last stanza of this passage is hortatory: "Believe me *Stella*" (67). Intent on his argument, perhaps for the moment more caught up in his own feelings than concerned for hers, he seems preoccupied with the process of persuasion whether that is what Stella needs or not. As if realizing that this style will not suffice in the end, he turns to an open and personal declaration of love.

The last lines of the poem (79–88) are both personal and bracing. The earlier teasing tone has accomplished its purpose by establishing perspective, but it has broken down under the weight of the occasion. The abstract reasoning of the central section has permitted the poet to work out a sensible, rational, and realistic source of comfort, but it has not fully answered the woman's need for love. In these last lines Swift not only admits the personal but insists upon it, repeating the pronouns "me" and "you" to define the human context.

> Me, surely me, you ought to spare,
> Who gladly would your Suff'rings share;
> Or give my Scrap of Life to you,
> And think it far beneath your Due;
> You, to whose Care so oft I owe,
> That I'm alive to tell you so.   (83–88)

The professions verge on the extreme, but they are expressed in simple, tonic phrases. Preceding them is a description of the kind of hard fact that requires Swiftian strength to face. Speaking of Stella and her friends, specifically himself, he says,

> Nor let your Ills affect your Mind,
> To fancy they can be unkind.   (81–82)

The extraordinary tacit realizations and admissions of these lines suggest the most unsentimental kind of observation and analysis.

Swift has here used poetry to work out a perspective from which he and Stella can look at the prospect of her death. Having made his emotions manageable, he has felt free to declare his love, the *raison d'être* of the poem. His struggle and its resolution may elicit from the reader an overwhelming sympathy, rather uncritical but entirely human. Along with the fear of desecrating the poem and the poet come other reasons for critical inhibition: the spareness; the almost prosaic quality; the realization that the poem is private and personal, rather than public and strategic; the sense that Swift is an honest and plain-speaking man—all make this, the best of Swift's poems to Stella, the most difficult to analyze.

Swift is not always so successful at presenting himself. The reader of "The Author upon Himself" (1714) may dislike the poem because he dislikes the Swift he meets there. Here the poet assumes the posture of a victim, claiming that Queen Anne, the Duchess of Somerset, and the Archbishop of York have conspired to ruin him. Though the stance is that of a victim, the voice is aggressive, self-pitying, and intensely righteous:

> BY an [old red-Pate, murd'ring Hag] pursu'd,
> A Crazy Prelate, and a Royal Prude.
> By dull Divines, who look with envious Eyes,
> On ev'ry Genius that attempts to rise;[8]　　　　　　　(1-4)

Self-compliment is heaped on self-compliment as Swift says he reconciled divinity and wit, moved and spoke with excessive grace, frequented the tables of the great, and managed to avoid the demeanor of a parson. And he does not redeem his unpleasantness with satiric wit, which has degenerated into sarcasm:

> S—— had the Sin of Wit no venial Crime;
> Nay, 'twas affirm'd, he sometimes dealt in Rhime:　　(9-10)

The lines lack humor and dignity as well as wit. With this tone Swift will not win the reader's trust or allay the nervousness he feels at the display of violent emotion.

As the poem continues, he makes an error in strategy by implying his own literary and political greatness rather than inventing an outside observer to comment on the power of his satire and the nobility of his goals. He comes forward himself to explain how St. John confides in him and how Harley passes over his superiors in rank to show him marks of favor:

> And, *Harley*, not asham'd his Choice to own,
> Takes him to *Windsor* in his Coach, alone.
> At *Windsor* S—— no sooner can appear,
> But, *St. John* comes and whispers in his Ear;　　(31-34)

Committing a sin more pedestrian than that of wit, he lets his speaker appear intolerably proud.

In an allusion to Milton, Swift suggests that his enemies are not real people subject to jealousy and spite, but mythic creatures of monumental evil. Just as Satan whispers in the ear of Eve, the Duchess of Somerset instills her venom into the royal ear. In a line that aims at noble resignation but conveys self-righteousness instead, Swift scorns inglorious flight and retires only after he has performed "what Friendship, Justice, Truth require" (73).

Everything verges on the extreme—the claims, the insults, the self-compliments. Swift is clearly not in control of the personality he presents. He wants to elicit pity and admiration, but he does not first take the precaution of convincing the reader that he deserves these responses, as a likeable, moderate man impelled to violence only by the intolerable vice of powerful criminals. The fault cannot lie in the themes or the goals, for these recur in Swift's imitation of Horace, Lib. 2. Sat. 6 ("I often wish'd, that I had clear"), written immediately after "The Author upon Himself," in 1714. Swift may have used the imitative form to curb his otherwise chaotic or unacceptable emotions. Imitation is always a useful means of control, and in this case the personality of the imitated poet has a chastening effect on the imitator.

From the Horatian satire Swift absorbs techniques for conveying humility. The ostensible humility masks the real greatness he wants to imply and makes it palatable. He casts himself from the first as the reluctant politician, the man great in spite of himself. All his desires center on his country estate, and he would be completely content if English politicians did not demand his service. He does not use his own voice to indicate their need for him. Instead, he records the rumor about their wishes that reaches his ears, treating ironically his "great importance" to the court:

> I must by all means come to Town,
> 'Tis for the Service of the Crown.   (13–14)

Or else he reproduces the demands in direct quotation:

> "*Lewis;* the *Dean* will be of Use,
> "Send for him up, take no Excuse."   (15–16)

The great politicians have no sense of the practical obstacles to Swift's coming. But he is presenting himself as a practical man, not a "great" one, and he resents the expense and the danger involved in traveling in England.

Once in England, another voice, not Swift's, implies he is a favorite:

> "Good Mr. *Dean* go change your Gown,
> "Let my Lord know you're come to Town." (23-24)

He visits Harley's levee, where a wag accuses him of pride. Far from being proud, he says he is perplexed, a plain man out of his element in a crowd of courtiers. With no feeling for courtly proprieties, he presses before his superiors in rank to show his love for Harley. Unlike "The Author upon Himself," where Swift seems to feel a certain glee over marks of distinction ("Admitted private, when Superiors wait," 30), the Horatian satire imputes his pushing to honest gaucherie. Harley's preference is briefly and delicately expressed ("I get a Whisper," 43), and voices other than Swift's confirm his importance by pleading for his interest in their causes. Modestly and with reluctance, he promises to do what he can.

The modesty implicit in these last lines becomes explicit in those that follow. Swift calls himself Harley's "humble Friend" (66), and truly what passes for conversation between them seems to contain little to be proud of. Cloistered in a coach, secure from prying eyes, the two exchange not state secrets but questions and answers about the time, the weather, and the passing chariots. They strain, with Beerbohmian ludicrousness, to read the words written underneath the country signs. This talk of trivia is far different from the portentous murmurs in "The Author upon Himself" ("But, *St. John* comes and whispers in his Ear," 34). Swift has not, however, given up his glory by association. The very triviality of the talk is a proof of real friendship and intimacy. With Swift, the great man is at ease.

By denying that anything special passes between him and Harley, he establishes for himself a level of social equality with the lord. The intimacy of two so distant in rank arouses envy. Swift anticipates, and so negates, what the splenetic will say:

"What, they admire him for his Jokes—
"See but the Fortune of some Folks!"   (87–88)

The end of the poem—a paean to his country seat, where he can escape from both the great and the envious—is probably misleading as a statement about how he preferred to live. The personality projected may not be biographically true, but it serves a purpose. It helps him convey his attitudes in a convincing and attractive manner.

Authors never falter so often as when they attempt to write about themselves. "The Author upon Himself" demonstrates the pitfalls. What is just praise in another's mouth is vanity and presumption in one's own. In his imitation of Horace, Lib. 2. Sat. 6., Swift avoids the difficulties by adopting the Horatian manner, as he does also in his imitation of Lib. 1. Epis. 7. ("*HARLEY,* the Nation's great Support," 1713). Other occasions require other precautions.

Critics have long puzzled over the question of vanity in "Verses on the Death of Dr. Swift, D.S.P.D. Occasioned by reading a Maxim in Rochefoulcault" (1731). At the time of its first publication, Swift's friends, especially Pope and William King, feared that the poem was vain and dishonest. With the approval of Pope, King produced a London edition that exised dangerous political references and, what is more, passages where Swift seemed to praise himself excessively and to contradict common views of his satiric practice. How could anyone believe that the poet "spar'd the Name" (460) when the very poem that makes the claim contains thirteen personal attacks? An accurate version, issued by Swift in Dublin, found its way through time to the eyes of Middleton Murry, whose strictures opened the modern phase of the controversy.[9] Maurice Johnson replied that the truth occupied a middle ground between self-condemnation and self-praise.[10] Barry Slepian retorted that Swift's eulogy was ironic.[11] Marshall Waingrow, whose essay has strongly influenced my work, fought valiantly to establish the end of the poem as a conventional apologia for satire.[12] And Arthur H. Scouten and Robert D. Hume, after carefully sifting through all the opinions, have concluded that the poem offers a "half-genuine apologia," which is deliberately exaggerated for the reader's comic delight.[13] What I want to investigate now is the importance of this self-portrait in eliciting and controlling the reader's trust.

The proem to "Verses on the Death of Dr. Swift," lines 1–72, moves rapidly and intricately, defining and redefining the object of satire. Swift says first that the "Fault is in Mankind" (4)—a statement so unspecific that it verges on blandness. His paraphrase of La Rochefoucauld's maxim immediately effaces this impression by speaking familiarly of "our" and "us"—of *our* blameworthy pleasure in distresses of *our* friends. The reader is to know from this point on that wherever else Swift directs his accusations, he will include himself. When the reader feels a blow, Swift will suffer too. What follows is a subtle interplay between the "you" of the poem, the reader, and the "I," the poet. *You* rebel against this maxim? *I* appeal for proof to reason and experience. *We all* resent the advancement of an equal. *I* love my friend as much as *you*, but would not have him higher than myself. (Similarly, *you* love your friend as much as *I*, but . . . ?)

Two entire stanzas regale "you," the reader, with tales of "your" resentment for superiors and patience in others' adversity. Resentment might begin to extend to Swift, so severe is the censure, except that he gives prompt relief by switching to the third person and to an example closer to his own case:

> WHAT Poet would not grieve to see,
> His Brethren write as well as he? (31–32)

The moment of respite continues. From the third person, author and reader move together to personification, apostrophe, and abstraction. The human race becomes again the primary object of satire, until Swift surprises the reader with an abrupt and jocular examination of his own envy:

> Give others Riches, Power, and Station,
> 'Tis all on me an Usurpation. (43–44)

The worst of it is, the author for the first time opposes himself directly to the reader: "Yet, when you sink, I seem the higher" (46). Does Swift view the reader, who has followed him trustingly thus far, as his antagonist? Would he reverse the meaning of the line and ascribe to one who has attended him so devotedly the same damnable degree of envy? Is the friendship to end here, *I* against *you* and *you* against *me*? Swift cuts off this line of questioning when he quickly redefines the "you." Instead of the reader, "you" comes to mean Pope or Gay or Arbuthnot or St. John. For the time, Swift takes all the blame, rallying himself for the envy he feels for his best friends. The penultimate stanza of the proem describes the blackest desecration of friendship. But the desecration is Swift's doing, and the reader sighs in relief.

The proem to "Verses on the Death of Dr. Swift" has established an alliance of poet and reader built upon trust. Swift has not exempted the reader from accusations implicit in the French maxim. To do so would hardly be consistent with his claim that envy is universal. He has embedded the accusations against "you" amid instances of his own culpability. He begins with "we," moves to "I," focuses momentarily upon "you," and then devotes stanza after stanza to self-blame. The reader sees that insofar as he stands charged, Swift shares in the indictment. Because the poet highlights and gives details of his own guilty feelings, the reader can more easily accept his position as "accomplice" or "accessory" to a more egregious criminal. Swift's honesty about himself and his disinclination to abuse the reader produce admiration and relief. The second part of the poem, lines 73–298, increases the sense of relief by showing the reader how much better off he is for his brief encounter with guilt than those who will not acknowledge guilt at all.

Swift's survey of all his "special Friends," as they react to his death, transfers the burden of the satire to persons remote from the reader. Those who remark his decline and foretell his death, those who receive the fatal news and treat with contempt his public bequest, his card-playing female acquaintances, his doctors and publishers, Lady Suffolk and the Queen, Chartres and Walpole, even Pope, Gay, Arbuthnot, and St. John—all these characters fall with utter unconsciousness into the posture described by La Rochefoucauld's maxim. Like Swift and the reader addressed in part one, they deserve blame for envying their friends. But unlike Swift, who has announced and insisted upon his guilt, and unlike the reader, with whom Swift has familiarly divided that guilt, they have no knowledge of their culpability. The reader of part two has the curious sensation of being privileged to bear blame under these circumstances. He may have resisted the first charges of envy, but he now recognizes that Swift has in fact honored him. Besides the tribute of a partnership with the poet, he has the glory of Swift's assumption that he sees his own faults clearly. How ridiculous, how hypocritical and deluded, is the position of those who congratulate themselves for pity they do not feel! How courageous, how insightful, is the position "we" share—that the "Fault is in Mankind," but that only a very few have the penetration to perceive it. The ladies who finger their diamonds and clubs, and lead a heart as they heartlessly dissect the dead Dean, have no edge over the honest, guilty reader.

Swift relies on his bond with the reader to enforce his central point: though all men consult their private ends, and all men should know themselves well enough to know that truth, their habitual selfishness need not preclude acts of public benefit. The phrase "private Ends," which occurs in Swift's paraphrase, is not in the original French maxim. It recurs in the lines that introduce part two, where he begins the discussion of his "special Friends." In opposition to that phrase stands "publick Uses"—the object of his final bequest and, as part three will show, the object of his life in general. His early insistence that he himself envies his friends and consults his private interests, in combination with his announcement of his disinterested public bequest, suggests that only those who recognize their culpability have the power to resist it. Only those who see that the fault is in themselves will sufficiently guard against it.

Swift has prepared the reader to receive this crucial point by continuously strengthening the bond between "us" and at the same time severing the connections between "us" and the rest of the blind world. The flattery succeeds wonderfully well as a strategy for convincing the reader to acknowledge and circumvent a habitual vice. The point itself is consistent with Swift's usual method of moral evaluation: he always stresses the overt action rather than the latent motive. Both *A Project for the Advancement of Religion* and *An Argument against Abolishing Christianity,* though not condoning hypocrisy, prefer it to unmasked vice. The closing eulogy, part three, may place a strain on the relationship, but it is typically Swiftian and carefully wrought.

The phrase "private Ends" occurs twice in the "impartial" speaker's eulogy of Swift. Without claiming that Swift never consulted his private interests (a claim that part one would clearly disprove), the first use of the phrase asserts that he could be altruistic:

> "He gave himself no haughty Airs:
> "Without regarding private Ends,
> "Spent all his Credit for his Friends:"   (330–32)

The phrase recurs when the speaker tells of the persecution Swift has endured from both foes and friends. Here it picks up the theme of La Rouchefocauld's maxim, expounded in part one and illustrated by specific examples in part two:

> "When, *ev'n his own familiar Friends*
> "Intent upon their private Ends;
> "Like Renegadoes now he feels,
> *"Against him lifting up their Heels."*   (403–06)

Swift is the only thoroughgoing altruist mentioned in this history of his career. As I have pointed out, he is also the only character in the poem who recognizes the temptations to selfishness. He does not exempt himself from temptation. Indeed, he has insisted upon his lapses from the first. But the eulogy shows how he has learned (and how the reader might learn after him) to leave a kingdom in his debt by facing up to a common human failing. Though vanity is present in the lines, mere vanity does not motivate them. Swift carries the reader with him toward self-knowledge. The eulogy no more serves an exclusive "private End" than Swift's actual favors for his friends or his verifiable efforts at promoting Irish self-sufficiency.

As for irony, those parts of the eulogy which deal with his political career appear to me straightforward. One might argue from "The Author upon Himself" that he was capable of at least slightly heavy-handed self-praise. One might choose to cite the letters. But why argue by analogy when the lines in question contain no ironic signals at all? Swift really did feel, and rightly, that he had been of use to friends and countrymen. On the other hand, when he speaks of his satire, one would expect a degree of irony. In almost all his work, he deprecates his role as satirist. He surely knew that he was stealing from Denham's elegy on Cowley the line "what he writ was all his own" (318). He surely knew what the reader knows from the poem itself: that he did not spare the name. These examples of irony suggest a spirit of play between the author and the reader, whose trust in Swift by this point should make him feel the vanity as the lightest of impositions and the irony as the most delightful of games. Swift's assertion that his satire deals only with correctable errors might seem ironic if left in isolation. But the lines that follow show that he is not thinking of the sweeping vices of *Gulliver's Travels* or "The Day of Judgement." He is thinking of physical defects and intellectual deficiencies unattended by pride:

"For he abhorr'd that senseless Tribe,
"Who call it Humour when they jibe:
"He spar'd a Hump or crooked Nose,
"Whose Owners set not up for Beaux.
"True genuine Dulness mov'd his Pity,
"Unless it offer'd to be witty." (465–70)

The vicious attacks on Pope's appearance might have crossed his mind at this moment in the writing. At any rate, the restraints suggested for satire are almost identical with those Swift recommends in the obviously straightforward verses "To Mr. Delany" (1718). Vanity and irony exist in this poem. They will not seduce the attentive reader from the crucial point or dissolve his relationship with the self-portraitist.

In the poems about himself—"The Author upon Himself," "I often wish'd, that I had clear," and "Verses on the Death of Dr. Swift"—the poet occasionally veers close to disaster but manages, for the most part, to keep his verses under control. The danger, however, is always imminent in Swift's poetry, even in the poems not primarily about himself. For since the reader is not thinking about form, his attention is drawn more directly to the speaker. How well Swift uses aspects of his personality as a rhetorical tool is therefore a legitimate concern of the critic. His other rhetorical strategies—his ways of reaching a friend or an enemy, his ways of reaching all mankind—are appropriate matters for analysis too and yield more of interest than studies of verse technique ("rhetorical strategies" used in a broad sense, meaning not figures of speech but methods of persuasion).

Swift's "Epistle to a Lady, Who desired the Author to make Verses on Her, in the Heroick Stile" (1733), written for Lady Acheson, illustrates the way his strategies work to reach his private friends and public enemies. He did not invent raillery, the most important of his methods for pleasing and persuading the lady, but the pose he cultivates to explain the raillery is largely an original creation. He plays an old curmudgeon, whose friends are to understand that he has a heart of gold and a habit of having all his whims indulged—a role he enjoyed in real life as well. Only such a man could write such a poem and expect to insinuate his advice in the guise of affectionate ribbing. Nor did Swift discover invective, the most important of his strategies for blackening the ministry. What he did discover was the usefulness of convincing the reader that he, a loving and lovable man, could be pushed into invective frenzy only by the most atrocious of crimes. Obviously, the two strategies, his particular brand of raillery and his particular brand of invective, work together to imply one pose and account for the double effect of the poem. Obviously, too, the pose tends to make him almost comic, as the good-natured man who believes in lighthearted laughter is transformed into the ferocious satirist. But the implied self-criticism does not weaken the point: Swift is not, like some of his fellow satirists, too proud to make fun of himself. It is another of his innovative strategies and is of prime importance in other works. His three intentions—to compliment and teach the lady, to censure Walpole, and to comment comically on his art—merge perfectly to form one of the best and most significant of his poems.

The poem begins abruptly, in the middle of a conversation. The lady has apparently asked Swift to write about her in heroic verse, assuming that the verse will be complimentary. He notices the assumption and pretends that the idea of praising her would never occur to him. He takes her request as an invitation to enumerate her faults (What's left? Do you want me to go over them *again*?) and protests that his criticisms are beginning to bore everyone around them. The lady replies ingenuously that he might praise her. In assuming her voice, Swift assumes a subtle defensive tone that shows off his skill at creating character through dialogue. In his own person, he has presented the lady's faults bluntly:

> Are you positive and fretful?
> Heedless, ignorant, forgetful?   (7–8)

The lady tries to extenuate her faults by periphrasis and qualification, while he gently mocks her attempts at evasion:

> If you think me too conceited,
> Or, to Passion quickly heated:
> If my wand'ring Head be less
> Set on Reading, than on Dress: (15–18)

Though Swift may tease his friend by making her sound evasive, he concedes to her some powerful arguments, which he only pretends to dismiss. Lady Acheson defends herself by citing mistakes in her upbringing that recall Swift's essay *Of the Education of Ladies* and his *Letter to a Young Lady, on her Marriage.* His opinions on the miseducation of women emerge to soften the poet's charge of ignorance without affecting the validity of his recommendations. The lady is still at fault for accepting her ignorance, but he has momentarily shifted the focus of his satire. Likewise, when the lady excuses her card-playing by citing the need to "drive out thinking" (86), she uses arguments that would have struck home to Swift. It was he, after all, who admired the slogan "Vive la bagatelle!" In real life, he might very well have shuffled off the excuse anyway, drawing a connection between the lady's illnesses and her cards. But it is convincing in context: it implies that he takes his friend seriously and analyzes her motives as carefully as he would his own.

He gives the lady her due not only by taking her excuses seriously, but by crediting her with important virtues. At first he puts the praise in her own mouth, but he does nothing to undercut it, and the reader is likely to accept her virtues as real. When the lady has rested her case, Swift pretends not to value her virtues even while he heaps more upon her:

THO' you lead a blameless Life,
Are an humble, prudent Wife;
Answer all domestick Ends,
What is this to us your Friends?

. . .

Tho' you treat us with a Smile,
Clear your Looks, and smooth your Stile:
Load our Plates from ev'ry Dish;
This is not the Thing we wish.   (99–102, 107–10)

The pose is transparent in one sense: Lady Acheson would know well enough that he was praising her. The indirection of the compliment, however, makes it less conventional and less like flattery. The grudging manner of delivering the compliment gives it a certain attractive twist, as though the truth were forcing him to praise his friend. Although the overall effect is teasing, it tends to compliment the lady too. We dare to talk this way only to people we love. The passage, then, conveys an indirect reassurance of Swift's affection and sets up, more effectively than outright praise, the criticism to come.

Swift really does have for the lady a serious lesson: she must learn in company to speak and listen to good sense. The crotchety pose serves the purposes of correction as well as compliment, for the poet bears part of the critical burden. The lady is truly at fault, but the poet may be overly particular. And he makes the criticism even more palatable by serving it up in the lady's own terms. He has in mind her personal and moral profit, but he makes it sound like a social duty. He says he takes his metaphors—meat and drink—from the philosophers, but the metaphors imply that speaking sensibly and listening to good sense are part of being a proper hostess. His emphasis seems to fall on the propriety of listening. Apparently the lady talks too much. The metaphor of carving, however, reverses the moral implications of the charge, so that the lady seems not selfish but self-defeatingly kind:

And, that you may have your Due,
Let your Neighbours *carve* for you.   (131–32)

Swift's raillery has been so affectionate, his criticism so careful, that no further concession to the lady is really necessary. But he has not yet answered her most serious objection to his style:

> Treat the Publick, and your Friends,
> Both alike; while neither mends.   (55–56)

The objection falls into two parts: that he treats his friends as badly as he treats politicians and that his satire is not reformative. In the last half of the poem, he attempts an answer that opens him to laughter and correction from his friend. In answering, he seizes the opportunity for some political hits and for a hard look at his art.

He admits that he treats his friends and his ministers in the same way. But the reader has had a practical demonstration of his skill at raillery and is unlikely to overlook the difference between that and the lines on government. Beginning in relative calm, the lines pick up speed and desperation, and the strength of the diction belies Swift's claim to "Mirth" and "Sport":

> Shou'd a Monkey wear a Crown,
> Must I tremble at his Frown?
> Could I not, thro' all his Ermin,
> Spy the strutting chatt'ring Vermin?
> Safely write a smart Lampoon,
> To expose the brisk Baboon?   (149–54)

If he feels scorn and not hate, it is scorn of an intense kind, and even that degree of distance is lost in the next stanza. With the image of the ship of state splitting on the rocks, he seems to lose his temper completely and reveals, in a parenthesis, how much Walpole and his crew can affect him:

> (Tho' it must be understood,
> I would hang them if I cou'd:)   (169–70)

In the last lines of the stanza, Swift rises to a crescendo of rage that his friend (rightly enough) finds incomprehensible. He has set up a series of expectations, only to violate them in the most obvious way. He has pretended to a detachment he cannot maintain. He tried to imply the triviality of his butts in words and rhythms that prove them not trivial. The comparison of Walpole to a schoolboy ready for whipping extends like a favorite fantasy and explodes in an ecstasy of revenge.

The lady is actually much closer to Swift's official position than he is himself, and she sees the contradictions in his attitude. To her, though not to him, the court quarrels are really insignificant; and she cannot understand why he should lose his temper and drop the thread of the discussion to "keep a Fuss" (187) with senates. Since he creates the lady's role, her words express his criticism of himself. Despite her rebuke, he reduces himself to absurdity by continuing to insist on his indifference to public affairs. This last and most positive insistence is possibly undercut by an allusion to a poem he may have written:

> (Sooner would I write in Buskins,
> Mournful Elegies on *Bluskins*)[14]

The fatuous claim to indifference merges with a serious discussion of Horace that bears no relation to the preceding satire on Walpole. The contrast between precept and practice is enforced by their juxtaposition. The terms in which Swift justifies Horatian satire, the claim that its effectiveness will excuse it, must apply only to his treatment of the lady, and not to his treatment of Walpole:

> THUS, I find it by Experiment,
> Scolding moves you less than Merriment.
>
>   . . .
>
> But, with Raillery to nettle,
> Set your Thoughts upon their Mettle: (207–08, 211–12)

Swift makes a convincing case for the reformative powers of laughing satire. He seems to believe, with Dryden, that the delicacy of Horatian cuts is simply more effective than the butchery of other satirists. But with Dryden, too, he seems to have a predilection for satiric butchery, whether effective or not. Dryden's tortured comparison of Horace and Juvenal betrays at once his real preference for Juvenal and his conviction that Horace is better.[15]

Swift confesses by self-ridicule that he cannot always write the kind of satire he recommends.

If his satire on Walpole is not Horatian, and if he excuses satire only on Horatian grounds, then the lady may win part of her quarrel. He has not proved that his political satire is reformative. The passages on public affairs suggest that he knows as much himself. He takes his doubts even further than his friend and hints that his political satire is reformative neither in motive nor in effect. The phrase "In a Jest I spend my Rage" (168) seems to imply that the motive for satire may be relief and not reform. The phrase "I would hang them if I could" (170) may suggest that his work is at least relatively futile. The references to the "Mirth" and "Sport" he finds in writing trivialize the motive and ignore the effect. His comparison of himself to the "Watermen of *Thames*" (165), hurling names at people as he rows by, may mean that he thinks his satire unjustified, vulgar, and ineffective. The reader is left to believe, perhaps as Swift himself believes, that satire can torture better than it can correct:

> And I find it answers right:
> Scorn torments them more than Spight. (145–46)

The "Epistle" ends with a return to the lady and a last word of explanation on why he must write satire: any heroic verse of his would either sound like satire or metamorphose to become satire. The need for explanation is a leitmotif that runs through the poem, but it does not account for all the involutions and implications. The "Epistle" is about Swift's reasons for rallying the lady, but it is also about his affection for her, his disgust with contemporary politics, and his doubts about his art.

In the verses on "The Day of Judgement" (1731?), Swift shapes his material to ensnare not private friends and public enemies, but mankind in general. Only the cleverest of readers will find his way out of the rhetorical trap. "*SATYR is a sort of Glass, wherein Beholders do generally discover every body's Face but their Own*," says Swift in the preface to *The Battle of the Books*.[16] At his best, however, he does not allow the reader to avoid self-knowledge. He refuses to form the conventional kind of satiric alliance, where the reader stands behind the writer, shielded, out of harm's way, and mocks all the fools the satirist points out. Fielding does not refuse the alliance. He encourages it in *Jonathan Wild,* for example, where he uses a completely transparent kind of irony that implies a league of all good men. The reader who understands the irony, and every reader does, is automatically included in the league. Gibbon does not refuse the alliance. He creates it in his famous chapters on Christianity, where the subtlety of his irony implies a league of the elite. The sophisticated reader who perceives the irony joins the author in ridiculing the dirty, foolish Christians. For Swift, however, these alliances circumvent the purpose of satire because for him satire works to reform the reader if it is to work at all.

Even in "Verses on the Death of Dr. Swift," where reader and poet seem nearly at one, Swift declines to protect his audience. He is always actively seeking to break down the conventional satiric alliance, to discourage the reader from assuming a safe position at his shoulder. His methods are many, but "The Day of Judgement" relies on the most effective he ever found. First, he makes sure the reader sees that every single human being is involved in the satiric damnation. Second, he includes himself in that damnation and so destroys the reader's only hope for protection. The sharing of guilt here is different from what it was in "Verses on the Death of Dr. Swift." There the poet's self-inclusion fostered trust, and the reader's position as accessory led to self-understanding. Here the poet uses his culpability to draw the reader to damnation. Though relying on more than one persuasive strategy, "The Day of Judgement" shows much more clearly than "Epistle to a Lady" the rhetorical effectiveness of satire on the satirist. When Swift "lashes first himself," as W. B. C. Watkins puts it,[17] the reader can hardly claim exemption from the satire or dissociate himself from the satirist on grounds that he is prideful or partial. When Swift acknowledges his own reflection, the world must see itself in the mirror:

WITH a Whirl of Thought oppress'd,
I sink from Reverie to Rest.
An horrid Vision seiz'd my Head,
I saw the Graves give up their Dead.
Jove arm'd with Terrors, burst the Skies,

And Thunder roars, and Light'ning flies!
Amaz'd, confus'd, its Fate unknown,
The World stands trembling at his Throne.
While each pale Sinner hangs his Head,
Jove, nodding, shook the Heav'ns, and said,
"Offending Race of Human Kind,
By Nature, Reason, Learning, blind;
You who thro' Frailty step'd aside,
And you who never fell—*thro' Pride;*
You who in different Sects have shamm'd,
And come to see each other damn'd;
(So some Folks told you, but they knew
No more of Jove's Designs than you)
The World's mad Business now is o'er,
And I resent these Pranks no more.
I to.such Blockheads set my Wit!
I damn such Fools!—Go, go, you're bit."

Whatever short-lived laughter "The Day of Judgement" may
evoke can scarcely survive a second reading. Such laughter has its
origin in the incongruity of low and lofty styles, as Swift adapts
his language to the different aspects of his Jove. The reader at first
associates the dream vision with serious religious works and prepares to accept it seriously. He perceives Jove as a combination of
traditional Christian and classically heroic elements, wielding his
thunderbolt and shaking the heavens with his nod. The phrasing in
the line "Amaz'd, confus'd, its Fate unknown" (7) even has a
Miltonic cast. Before Jove stand the pale sinners, appropriately
terrified and appropriately ashamed. But Jove's first words detract
from his dignity and change the heroic to the mock-heroic in the
reader's retrospect.

Jove's first witticisms—his first departures from divine decorum—are funny and not altogether disconcerting. As he continues
his verbal play, however, his cleverness becomes cumulatively
sinister and offensive, unbecoming a god. He is playing when he
attributes "never falling" to the pride which caused, in part, the
Fall. The whole joke involved in the equivalency of falling and
never falling contributes to the reader's unease. Jove plays, likewise, with the idea that blindness, and not insight, proceeds from
nature, reason, and learning. At the same time, he mocks the most

cherished eighteenth-century ideals. The colloquial tone reaches its fullness when he ceases to speak of himself as "Jove" and comes in his own person to damn, resent, and set his wit against the fools. The smug and colloquial parenthesis ("So some Folks told you," 17) has prepared for the shift to "I resent" (20) and "I damn" (22). The use of the first person prepares in turn for the culmination of the witticisms—the execrable play on *damn*. "God damn you," Jove is saying. "Go to hell." When the reader remembers that it was Swift who loved a "bite" more than any other form of joking, then Jove's announcement that he and the churches have duped the poor sinners ("Go, go, you're bit," 22) sounds very like a satirist's crude dismissal. The curse, on second reading, becomes the secularized swearing of a frustrated reformer.

The descent from the heroic to the colloquial and clever may provoke the reader's early laughter, but he will find in the cleverness of Jove grounds for Swift's real horror and, at the last, grounds for horror of his own. The god who sets his wit against mankind and speaks in Swift's own idiom is the satirist writ large. He dramatizes the problems of satire—the problems, in particular, which interested Swift himself. Jove-the-satirist fulfills the traditional desires of his human counterpart. From his omnipotence proceeds a measure of detachment, and he feels only resentment at the "Pranks" (20) of men. From his omnipotence likewise proceeds his effectiveness in attack, and he may choose to annihilate man with the assurance that he can implement his choice. The human satirist longs to see the objects of his hatred as trivial. At the same time, he longs for the power to attack and obliterate.

But if Jove has successfully detached himself from human folly and spared himself the *saeva indignatio* that tortured a Juvenal or a Swift, he has little motive for annihilating man. Outside the scheme of the poem, the question may not occur. God may damn the fools because they deserve damnation, though he feels not even resentment. Within the scheme of the poem, however, Jove refers not to the principles of justice and desert, but only to his own feelings. The race offends him personally, and personally he resents it. His resentment, as a motive, cannot satisfy the reader, but it is the only motive he offers.

The human satirist, on the other hand, finds his motive in the savage indignation that belies his conventional pretense to detachment. When the detached Jove damns all mankind, he raises questions about the motives of his counterpart—but in this case, only by implication, because his counterpart can never be detached. Jove raises questions, then, not about what the satirist is but about what he would be if he could realize at once his desires for detachment and for effectiveness in attack.

Jove chooses to destroy man in demonstrating his effectiveness. He saves none, though presumably he might have exercised his omnipotence in the process of salvation. As a superhuman satirist, the character here suggests that Swift shares with his opponents real doubts about satire: satire may be primarily destructive, and not reformative, in its motivation. The "Epistle to a Lady" contains the same suggestion. Swift pretends to Horatian calm until his anger asserts itself and he tells what he would do if he but had the power:

> Safe within my little Wherry,
> All their Madness makes me merry:
> Like the Watermen of *Thames,*
> I row by, and call them Names.
> Like the ever-laughing Sage,
> In a Jest I spend my Rage:
> (Tho' it must be understood,
> I would hang them if I cou'd:)   (163–70)

In "The Day of Judgement," the satirist can laugh and hang them too.

The reader cannot expect Swift-the-dreamer—the speaker of the poem—to perceive and decry the implications for satire that derive from the character of Jove. If the "I" were Swift-the-satirist, in fact, he might take pleasure in the vision because it fulfills the satirist's fondest wishes. The dreamer may perceive, however, the horror of his own predicament. When Jove damns all mankind without exception, the dreamer is drawn from his point of observation into the mass of the damned. He, too, has come to see his fellows damned, only to meet with damnation himself. He, too, in the course of the poem, has speculated on Jove's designs until he has come to the inevitable conclusion: the Swiftian Jove will damn the Swiftian dreamer. Swift in one of his aspects will pass judgment on Swift in another.

No less must the reader acknowledge his presumption and self-delusion. He has expected from the first of the poem an apocalyptic vision—a sky rent in two and pale sinners before a godlike God. The "horrid Vision" (3) humiliates the reader because it disappoints his literary and his religious expectations. That humiliation prepares him for another. The poem compels him to accept as his judge a god who cares nothing about his human dignity or his due process. The curious changes in tense throughout the poem extend the implications to the whole "Offending Race," as well as indicate the state of timelessness appropriate to the Day of Judgment. On that day the reader finds no exception made for anyone, whatever his time or place. His only hope for escape would lie in alliance with the poet, but he cannot appeal to the poet because Swift has come from his point of vantage to join the pale sinners himself. The reader must submit, with Swift, to the judgment of an imperious Jove—a Jove who shares some characteristics with Swift as satirist and who emanates from the imagination of the Swift who dreams.

Because it handles the reader so expertly, "The Day of Judgement" is a study in rhetorical excellence, and because of that, the poem is flawed. The flaw is a function of the poet's expertise. The reader can deflect the satire, to an extent, by pure admiration of the skill. When his aesthetic interest in the poem outweighs his moral interest, the balance of his attention shifts from profit to pleasure. The better the poem, the more pleasure it gives him. That is why the clever reader runs the risk of learning little from a poem like this.

What distinguishes the poetry from the prose, which is also rhetorically rich? What makes a discussion of the poetry useful as distinct from a discussion of the prose? The answers are several, but two stand out. Swift seems to allow himself greater emotional latitude in his poems: his hatred is more virulent, his love more intense. Second, his tools for expressing these emotions are frequently more varied and subtle. However much he may have disdained some poetic conventions, he uses others in exceedingly interesting ways. The following chapters of this book will deal with groups of poems that owe their value to a comfortable combination of original and conventional. A discussion of the poetry in terms of rhythm—a strong point of Swift's—will form a suitable prelude. I have said that the poems are not usefully approached by analyzing caesuras. On the other hand, this poet is adept at handling the broader aspects of rhythm—meter and variations upon a metrical scheme—and makes his skill known. With regard to rhythm broadly considered, and Butler's octosyllabic rhythm in particular, he is original even in his use of convention. The unorthodox uses he finds for rhythm and the changes he made in Samuel Butler's line show off his flair for invention almost as well as his purely Swiftian strategies. Though he is doing more recasting than discovering, we are here, as everywhere, surprised by his boldness. Sometimes the rhythms contrast ironically with the subject matter. Octosyllabics, carrying inevitable associations with Butler, give a special flavor to the Stella poems. Sometimes, as in the "Legion Club" (1736) and "Helter Skelter," the rhythms are startlingly imitative.

In "Helter Skelter, Or The Hue and Cry after the Attornies, going to ride the Circuit" (1731), Swift uses a meter atypical for him: the trochaic. An inversion in the initial stress of an iambic foot, says Jespersen, creates the stress pattern 4-3-1-4 or 4-2-1-4 in the first four syllables, where the numbers indicate the strength of stress. Because the second syllable is stronger than the third, the ear is surprised only at first, in only one place out of ten. When the inversion occurs elsewhere in the line, it always follows a pause, so the state of surprise to the ear is exactly the same as in the case of initial inversion. With iambic inversion in a trochaic line, however, when 1-4 substitutes for 4-1, "we have the disagreeable clash of two strong syllables, further, we have two disappointments per line."[18] The trochaic line is therefore extremely inflexible, and its inflexibility can give the impression of mechanical motion, like a toy mouse running across a floor.

For "Helter Skelter," Swift capitalizes on the mechanical quality of the trochaic rhythm to make young attorneys seem subhuman, without natural life. The long list of their apparel and appurtenances reinforces the effect of the mechanical meter, and the repetition adds to the sense of motion without life:

And with Harness-Buckles furnish'd;
And with Whips and Spurs so neat,
And with Jockey-Coats compleat;

And with Boots so very grazy
And with Saddles eke so easy
And with Bridles fine and gay,
Bridles borrow'd for a Day,
Bridles destin'd far to roam,
Ah! never to return Home;   (8–16)

The rhythm is hypnotic, and we are betrayed into taking the elements of the description as if they were of equal value—contemptible in an amusing way. The mention of borrowed bridles, destined never to return home, seems like one more item in the jogging list, but it is more. Swift delights here in jolting us with aspects of his serious indictment when we would be content to sleep the poem away. He proceeds to details of caps and wigs that are innocuous enough, and then inserts "Cambrick Ruffles not their own" (20). He amplifies this sinister note with a description of the lawyers' shirts, which look as if they belong to their betters. A few more lines of hypnotic blandness, and we discover that these men of law are thieves, having stolen from hostess, barber, cutler, soldier, sutler, vintner, and tailor. The victims fall into another rhythmic and inevitable list that has as much impact at first as a recitation of "Doctor, Lawyer, Indian-Chief." But they are real victims with real grievances, and we wake at least long enough to notice that these lawyers have some law but no sense of justice (31), live on public bounty (38), engage in plunder and pillage (40), and murder equity (49). We realize that we have been sleeping through a description of actual crime, like "the People" who have remained inert and immobile while the criminals went about their work:

All to murder Equity,
And to take a double Fee;
Till the People all are quiet
And forget to broil and riot,   (49–52)

We wake to the perception that these riders are mounted on the backs of their clients and their country.[19] Of course, the rhythm has a fascination of its own, independent of what it does to the subject matter. The fascination certainly operates on the reader, and it probably operated on Swift, whose interest in rhythmic experimentation anticipated the adventures of Auden, as well as of lesser nineteenth and twentieth-century writers, like Thomas Moore and Bret Harte.

From the swirling dimeter and wild rhymes of "The Description of an Irish Feast, translated almost literally out of the Original Irish" (1720), to the long, irregular, and prosy line of "Mrs. Harris's Petition" (1701) to the anapestic variation of "The Grand Question debated. Whether Hamilton's Bawn should be turned into a Barrack or a Malt-House" (1729), the frequency of Swift's experiments show his continuing preoccupation with this aspect of his art. But the new uses he found for the octosyllables of Samuel Butler must, above all, establish his skill at poetic bravura. His development of Butler's practices in several respects, rhythmic and otherwise, proves he could make the right materials into something truly Swiftian.

External evidence for assuming that Butler influenced Swift consists entirely in a dubious anecdote of the dubious Letitia Pilkington. She claimed that *Hudibras* was Swift's favorite reading, that he practically knew it by heart. Nowhere in his correspondence does he mention Butler, but *Hudibras* may well have been the most popular poem of the Restoration, and Swift lived half his life as a Restoration man. He could hardly have failed to know *Hudibras* even if he had not found attractive Butler's distrust of reason, his views on monarchy, his hatred of dissenters, his contempt for lawyers, and his skepticism about the new science. Because he shared all these attitudes with Butler, he had more reason to pick up pointers from him. Internal evidence shows that he did, though he returned to posterity, with interest, the little that he borrowed from Butler.

Swift's poetic allusions to Butler are few but unmistakable. In "Baucis and Philemon" (1708-9), he quotes a line from Butler almost verbatim, and he recalls lines from his predecessor in "Epistle to a Lady."[20] He may even have got several hints from Butler for use in his prose. He may have drawn his title for *A Discourse Concerning the Mechanical Operation of the Spirit* from these lines in *Hudibras*:

With Crosses, Relicks, Crucifixes,
Beads, Pictures, Rosaries and Pixes:
The Tools of working out Salvation,
By meer Mechanick Operation.[21]

Before Swift wrote *The Mechanical Operation* or "A Digression on Madness," Butler advanced the idea that one man's flatulence is another man's spirituality (II.iii.773-76). Swift's Laputans, who eat food cut into geometrical shapes and tailor clothing with the help of a quadrant and compasses, might have taken form when he read Butler's lines on telling time by algebra and measuring ale by geometry (I.i.119–26).

Swift's and Butler's jokes about mathematicians show their mutual loathing for pedantry. Swift condemned it all his life, beginning with the "Ode to The Honourable Sir William Temple" (1692), where he castigated ill-mannered scholars. Butler parodies astrological cant and scientific jargon in the speeches of Sidrophel and Wachum—speeches that recall, with their Venus's and Mars's and oppositions and benignities, passages from Jonson's *Alchemist*. Legalism and Aristotelian logic-chopping are ridiculed in passages like the dispute between Hudibras and Ralpho about the respective merits of synods and bears. The Puritans, with their "out-goings" and "vessels" and "dispensations" and "new light," come under continuous attack.

Swift's and Butler's dislike of pedantry, one abuse of reason, extends to other aspects of reason as well. "A Digression on Madness" shows that Swift distrusts both ratiocination and its frequent product, ideology. He is a special kind of antirationalist, who alternately touts common sense and Platonistic Reason. Ralpho's remarks to Hudibras about learning as a cobweb in the brain that blocks the avenues to truth and makes plain things intricate, prove that Butler subscribes to this indictment of misused reason (I.iii.1337–40, 1349–54).

Among the general resemblances between Swift and Butler, however, the most important for this study is the similarity of their views on poetry. They seek to give their poems a fresh aspect by showing how the old conventions reek. In "Stella's Birth-Day. A great Bottle of Wine, long buried, being that Day dug up" (1723), Swift makes fun of inspiration by giving a bottle of wine all the divine power of the muses. Butler uses the same device for the same purpose when he invokes an alcoholic muse at the beginning of *Hudibras:*

> Thou that with Ale, or viler Liquors,
> Didst inspire *Withers, Pryn,* and *Vickars,*
> And force them, though it were in spight
> Of nature and their stars, to write;
>
>   . . .
>
> Assist me but this once, I 'mplore,
> And I shall trouble thee no more.   (I.i.639–42, 657–58)

The difference between the two authors is as striking as the similarity. Whereas Swift everywhere dissociates himself from bad poetry and tries to offer a genuine alternative to atrophied verse, whereas he seldom, even in jest, compares himself to poetic hacks, Butler invokes the muse of notoriously bad poets.

Butler appears to take poetry in general, and his own poetry in particular, much less seriously than Swift. The charge of casualness, so frequently leveled at Swift, is more appropriately applied to Butler. He commonly underlines a digression by saying the equivalent of "Let's get back to the point," a proof of self-confidence that Swift could not have risked. He even acknowledges the bane of the couplet-maker in lines that implicate himself:

> But those that write in *Rhime,* still make
> The one *Verse,* for the others sake:
> For, one for *Sense,* and one for *Rhime,*
> I think's sufficient at one time.   (II.i.27–30)

The freedoms Butler takes with poetry reminds one more of Byron than of Swift. Nevertheless, they provide a possible source for Swift's occasional *pose* of casualness and for his remarks about the "trifling" nature of his poems.

Both Swift and Butler pervert mythology to mock old-fashioned poetic decoration. In "Apollo Outwitted. To the Honourable Mrs. Finch, under her Name of Ardelia" (1709), Swift writes about a droll confrontation between the sun god and Mrs. Finch:

OVID had warn'd her to beware,
    Of Stroling God's, whose usual Trade is,
Under pretence of Taking Air,
    To pick up Sublunary Ladies.   (21-24)

Not only the rhyme but the comic debasement of the gods reminds us of Butler. The most famous simile in *Hudibras* follows
the same comic pattern, though compared to Swift's charming
lines it suffers from archness:

The Sun had long since in the Lap
Of *Thetis,* taken out his *Nap,*
And like a *Lobster* boyl'd, the *Morn*
From *black* to *red* began to turn.   (II.ii.29-32)

Notable in these two authors is the lack of acrimony toward
myth. The affectionate transformation of myth shows that neither
hates it in itself, perhaps because they associate it with the classical poetry they both admire. What they do hate is the eternal
re-use of old conventions without humorous alteration. By adapt-
ing myth to their own comic purposes, they cast a satiric light on
modern poets who simply retail classic material.

Common sense is the ultimate poetic standard for Swift and
Butler. Both inveigh against the distortion of reality usual in contemporary verse. When Swift takes poets to task for lying or for
writing what is blatantly implausible, he comes very close to
Butler. For both poets the falsification of a lady's character in
love poetry is a flagrant instance of poetic lying. Butler claims, as
Swift does, that praise in love verse is grossly unrealistic. In the
widow's words:

Some with *Arabian spices* strive
T'embalm her, cruelly alive;
Or *season* her, as *French* Cooks use,
Their *Haut-gusts, Boullies,* or *Ragusts;*
Use her so barbarously ill,
To grind her Lips upon a *Mill,*
Until the *Facet Doublet* doth
Fit their *Rhimes* rather than her mouth;   (II.i.595-602)

Saccharine poems about real women are bad enough, but lovely lines about truly vicious women, the poets agree, are even worse. Butler says that poets would kick in prose the women they adore in rhyme (II.i.622). In the verses "To Stella, Who Collected and Transcribed his Poems" (1720), Swift describes fair Chloe drinking downstairs with the footmen, Silvia expiating her whorishness in Bridewell, Phillis mending holes in smocks, and Iris suffering from syphilis (39–48).

Though the points of the Butler and Swift passages are identical, the comparative mildness of Butler is typical of the difference between the two writers. Where Swift would rise to the highest pitch of anger, Butler makes a joke. Swift's lines are full of coarse and specific portraits. When Butler does use images to paint a picture, he uses them humorously, without the drive toward degradation that characterizes Swift. We see the difference in tone even more sharply because Butler, like Swift, chooses his images from everyday life. Ian Jack has compiled a list of typical Butlerian images: " 'Out-of fashion'd Cloaths', bowls, watches that go 'sometime too fast, sometime too slow', 'a Candle in the Socket', and beer 'by Thunder turn'd to Vinegar'." [22] A similar list for Swift might include a pendulum, a vomiting drunkard, meat, a dammed-up stream gathering chaff, the sea, "Porters o're a Pot of Ale," tradesmen showing their worst wares first, a tavern sign, and a rabbit hunt. Both writers tend to concentrate on images from animals. At first glance, the images of Swift and Butler are very much alike. Yet, as one notices the difference in motive for using a figure, he will feel that Butler's images are compelling, ingenious, and memorable; that Swift's are pallid, negligent, and forgettable. Butler does much more with his images than Swift. He draws them out, develops them, transforms them. He seems to think of one image, he effortlessly changes to another, and then he takes it through several different turns. When he speaks of "new light," the implications burgeon as the metaphors unfold:

A Light that falls down from on high,
For Spiritual Trades to cousen by:
An *Ignis Fatuus,* that bewitches,

And leads men into Pools and Ditches,
To make them *dip* themselves, and sound
For Christendome in Dirty pond;
To dive like Wild-foul for Salvation,
And fish to catch Regeneration.   (I.i.501–08)

The static images of Swift show no such ingenuity. For protean imagery resembling Butler's, one must turn to Swift's prose, for example to the manic *Tale of a Tub*. In verse Swift's technical superiority to his predecessor has other sources.

The "hudibrastics" of Sir John Mennes and Dr. James Smith in *Musarum Deliciae* (1656) and *Wit Restored* (1658) were popular before Butler wrote his masterpiece. But as Ehrenpreis notes, Swift's age by and large associated this couplet with *Hudibras,* not with the comic Mennes and Smith or the serious Milton and Marvell.[23] Swift probably had Butler in mind when he chose the octosyllabic couplet for over half his poems. What he added was a flexibility of rhythm that reflected his greater flexibility of tone. Butler almost always fails when he tries to render speech. Here he imitates an exhausted messenger:

That beastly Rabble,—that came down
From all the Garrets—in the Town,
And Stalls, and Shop-boards—in vast swarms,
With new-chalk'd Bills—and rusty Arms,   (III.ii.1505–08)

Swift would never have let a mechanical device like punctuation substitute for variety and subtlety. His poems "Horace, Epist. I. VII" ("*HARLEY*, the Nation's great Support," 1713) and "An Apology to the Lady C—R—T" (1725) show what a brilliant impersonator can do with a relatively rigid metric scheme.

Swift almost never distorts the emphases or syntax of natural speech, even when he is not imitating dialogue. Butler sometimes takes ear-splitting liberties with stress:

I'l stake my *self* down against you: (II.i.294)

In times of *Peace,* an *Indian,*   (II.ii.418)

And the reader can get hopelessly tangled in his syntax:

> Detect lost *Maidenheads,* by sneezing,
> Or breaking wind, of *Dames,* or pissing.   (II.iii.285–86)

Swift enjambs his lines, and with some frequency, but his enjambments are never jarring. Butler's may startle the reader past the point of enjoyment:

> Whether a *Pulse* beat in the black
> List, of a Dappled *Louse's* back: .   (II.iii.305–06)

Swift contributed to the octosyllabic line sophistication, grace, and subtlety. Despite their roughness, Butler's lines are monotonous. Despite the monotony, they are hard on the ear.

In departing from the example of his predecessor, Swift did not reject all his comic devices. He probably drew inspiration from Butler for the odd rhymes he loved so well. Butler's facility at this is too well known to need documentation. In games with Sheridan, for example, Swift cultivated the talent until it approached Butler's. He was prodigiously proud of the rhyme *"Bettesworth"* and "Sweat's Worth" in his verses "On the Words—Brother Protestants, and Fellow Christians" (1733), and various stories emerged to explain how he arrived at it. But he did not want to adopt an exclusively comic tone, so he did not consistently use such devices.

Butler's speciality is farce. He is almost never tender, and he is almost never fierce. Typical of his humor is the comedy of Part I, Canto I, where Hudibras, in a lengthy stanza, tries to mount his horse. In the same farcical mood, Butler describes how the widow inveigles the knight into claiming that he has a tail. Two or three passages might serve to support the notion that Butler can be "elegant" or "lyrical," but in each case the larger farce really determines the mood. (Hudibras, for example, can profess love eloquently enough, but we know that the speeches are hypocritical.) Swift could not have drawn upon Butler for his variety of tone, just as he could not have looked to him for metrical variety.

Swift seldom drew obviously on other writers. He prided himself on his originality. The difficulty of authenticating a clear debt to Butler proves this very point, and almost every other creditor of Swift's runs an equal risk of not getting paid—even in the small change of criticism. The influence of the classical poets is, as an exception, easy to trace. The titles of the Horatian imitations betray their origin right away. The two "Descriptions" clearly depend upon Virgil. The whole of "Baucis and Philemon" is indebted to Ovid. The French moralists, more than the French poets, must have had an effect on Swift. He was proud to identify himself with La Rochefoucauld and began what may be his greatest poem ("Verses on the Death of Dr. Swift") with one of the Frenchman's maxims. He may have found inspiration in the fables of La Fontaine and reinforcement for his own high standards in the tough moral tradition of Pascal and La Bruyère. Among French poets he extolled Voiture for skill at raillery in the verses "To Mr. Delany." The witty, courtly, rakish Voiture could appeal to one side of Swift's nature.

But the English influences are harder to identify. Swift's general debts are subtle and his specific allusions rare. The odes show what he read and liked as an immature poet, but he largely turned against the styles he imitated in them. The parodies show what he read and hated in early and contemporary poetry, but the alternatives he seems to propose have no clear relationship to the work of other men. Harold Williams' book on the contents of Swift's library gives a list of what he owned. He was interested enough in works by Garth, Pope, Marvell, and Cotton to annotate certain lines; he probably owned a Shakespeare; he collected poems by Spenser, Milton, Waller, Cowley, Wycherley, Gay, Parnell, and Prior.[24] Williams quietly concludes that Swift's collection of the English poets could hardly be called comprehensive. Swift was not concerned to build up, for possible reference, a library of English verse. The list of books he owned proves little about the books that actually influenced him. Even that little comes under suspicion, for some of the books were gifts from friends.

The letters provide some evidence for what he liked in verse. They prove, for example, that he read sympathetically the work of James Thomson, though he never owned a copy.[25] But Swift never hints that Thomson or anyone else affected his own writing. In the poems themselves one finds here and there a few specific references to other English authors—a line from Garth, an idea from Cowley. These obviously mean very little about Swift's development as a poet. Where are the broad influences that shape every significant poet's work? Was Swift essentially a poet *sui generis,* or did the older poets have a substantial effect on him?

I would argue that neither Swift nor any other man could develop a skill at poetry without drawing upon the experience of other poets. However unconventional, however antipoetic Swift may seem, he was subject to the currents that swept over the literary men of his time. From Dryden he might have learned something of a conversational style. From Cotton, he might have gathered the possibilities of coarse comedy in octosyllabic verse. Cotton's vulgarity in the *Virgil Travestie*

> *I Sing the Man* (read it who list,
> A Trojan true as ever pist,)[26]

sometimes recalls the Swiftian vulgarity of a poem like "The Problem" (1699). From Oldham, Swift might have picked up pointers about satiric ferocity, though Oldham is much more heavy-handed and single-toned. Like Swift, Oldham indulges in cruel visions of revenge. Here is the Restoration poet, in the second satire "Upon the Jesuits," suggesting that each shire bring in a certain quota of priests:

> And let their mangled quarters hang the isle
> To scare all future vermin from the soil.[27]

Compare the sadism in Swift's "Legion Club."

Ben Jonson's career paralleled Swift's in several ways. His verses "On the Famous Voyage" may have provided Swift with an excremental ancestor, and the poem seems to anticipate some of Swift's preoccupations in the "Description of a City Shower" (1710). His "Execration upon Vulcan" shows a delight in name-calling that Swift would have appreciated. His satiric anger approaches Swiftian rage. His love poetry operates outside the Petrarchan conventions. His success in each poetic genre, like Swift's, depends largely on his command and manipulation of the reader's trust. And his lack of "yield" when analyzed by New

Critical methods makes him Swift's fellow in scholarly neglect.

Butler provided Swift with a verse form and comic rhymes, but he had little to teach him about tone. Rochester might have supplied some of the deficiency with his skill at satiric invective. Donne and Marvell might have helped Swift express the other side of his nature, his affectionate honesty with women. In later chapters we will look at Swift's variations in tone, comparing him with Rochester, Donne, and Marvell. Tracing such analogues affords a perspective, but it does not open up a new field for criticism. Swift *might* have learned from others. That is all the critic can say with certainty. Beside the borrowings of his contemporaries, his debts are negligible. In the Augustan Age, of all periods, his poetic contribution was strikingly original.

The apparent spareness of Swift's verse—a spareness of allusion and of device—closes off to the critic some common avenues of research. At the same time, his nearness to the surface of his poems, his rhetorical complexity, and his experiments with a few poetic conventions open other prospects. How well Swift uses aspects of his personality to control the reader's response, how well his strategies work to involve the reader in the satire and break down the traditional satiric alliance, how well his rhythms reinforce his meaning—these are exciting subjects for critical inquiry. Whatever his lack of skill in other aspects of poetry—or rather, however strong his disdain for them—his facility in what he does do proves him an indispensable poet. He cared enough about poetry proper, apart from bows toward predecessors and other poetic conventions, to work at developing an outstanding original talent. The poems that resulted are not expendable. Anyone who thinks so should try imitating them. By the force of his projected personality and the richness of his satiric experience, Swift does things with poetry that other poets simply cannot do.

2. Poems on Poetry

In the uncommon field of Swift's poetry, scholarship commonly holds that Swift never claimed to be either a poet or a critic of poetry. What he wrote in verse (his "antipoetry," according to this view) represents an extreme example of reaction against the heroic or romantic attitude toward the poet and his art. Pope regarded poetry as a sacred calling and himself as a young priest, but Swift never indulged in this kind of sacerdotal daydream. How could anyone imagine that the satirist who let fly at kings, ministers, and established scholars would have bowed before the poet's less palpable glory? No, all Swift's works evidence his disrespect for the conventions of poetry—from the *Discourse Concerning the Mechanical Operation of the Spirit,* where poetic inspiration is derived from the "hexagonal morsure" of little animals upon certain capillary nerves, to the excremental poems, where poetic cant is debunked, to the Stella poems, those triumphs over the human urge for poetic sentiment.

Herbert Davis began this critical trend in his fine pioneering essay, "Swift's View of Poetry." The few other critics who have generalized about Swift's poetry, who have not limited themselves to the relatively safe province of a particular poem or group of poems, have tended to assume his conclusions. Their arguments leave one with the impression that Swift's contempt is not confined to bad poetry or heroic poetry, but extends to poetry itself. This outcome is hardly surprising, given the assumption that Swift never wanted to be a poet, but it has dangerous consequences. Who will dare to treat the poetry with respect when the poet himself is derisive?

To take a writer seriously when he shows outright contempt for what he is doing is to flout his authority in a particularly egregious way. The case is made worse by Swift's habitual taunting of critics. The learned reader, he says in *A Tale of a Tub,* can ferret out enough material here to keep him occupied for the rest of his life. In the verses "On Poetry: A Rapsody" (1733), he suggests that commentators see more in Homer than Homer ever knew himself. The contempt Swift shows for criticism and the apparent disdain he has for poetry make the criticizing of his poetry seem like farcical business. That is one reason why his poetry is criticized so seldom.

Swift's contempt for critics will undoubtedly haunt them forever, but his disdain for poetry is hardly clear-cut enough to justify all this inhibition. A survey of the evidence indicates that he despised bad poetry and poetic cant and all the worn-out paraphernalia of poetic convention. In certain limited respects and for reasons peculiarly his own, he also looked down on the poet. But he did not find poetry itself contemptible. The common view fails to distinguish between Swift's attitude toward the poet and his attitude toward poetry. It fails likewise to distinguish between his attitude toward poetry and his feelings about bad verse, especially when decked out in hackneyed heroic ornaments. The failure to make these distinctions can only obscure some important facts. Swift *was* a poet. He *knew* he was a poet. The critic may have to adjust to Swift's special brand of poetry, but he need not feel intimidated by his apparent casualness.

The verses "On Poetry" help to clarify Swift's views of the poet, of bad poetry, and of heroic poetry. Indirectly they show as well what he wanted good poetry to do. The subtitle, "A Rapsody," should warn the reader that the poem is satire, a "rapp" being a counterfeit coin as well as a blow to the head. It refers primarily, however, to the expectations of Swift's audience, expectations that he intends to foil. The poet who writes on poetry is supposed to rhapsodize. The heroic poet might lay claim to divine inspiration or a heavenly mission. Swift carefully constructs the beginning of the poem so that it alternately elicits and thwarts the old heroic responses. Instead of a panegyric on poetry in the tradition of Milton and Dryden, the reader finds a satire on poetry in the tradition of Oldham and Rochester.

From heroic generalization, one dips into vulgarity, then reascends to heroic heights, only to pick up momentum for the fall in the third stanza:

> Not Beggar's Brat, on Bulk begot;
> Nor Bastard of a Pedlar *Scot*;
> Nor Boy brought up to cleaning Shoes,
> The Spawn of *Bridewell*, or the Stews;
> Nor Infants dropt, the spurious Pledges
> Of *Gipsies* littering under Hedges,
> Are so disqualified by Fate
> To rise in *Church*, or *Law*, or *State*,
> As he, whom *Phebus* in his Ire
> Hath *blasted* with poetick Fire.   (33–42)

Against what is Swift directing all this alliterative, spitting contempt? The first object of attack is clearly the society that favors the undeserving and mistreats the poet. But aside from the bitter anger at contemporary treatment of poets, the opening stanzas imply that Swift feels contempt for the poet himself—for any poet in the present age. The whole beginning of the poem explores this paradox: whereas every fool wants to write poetry, only a fool would want to be a poet. The writing of poetry involves almost insuperable difficulties. Not empire, nor lawmaking, nor science requires such enormous resources "As how to strike the *Muses Lyre*" (32). And what is the poet's reward? In Swift's exaggerated terms, bastards are better qualified for advancement.

As the verses proceed, Swift makes his poet at once admirable and ridiculous—the one because he is above (or at least incompetent at) the vices of his age, and the other because he writes for no earthly reason whatever. The pleasure of self-expression would not occur to an eighteenth-century man writing on poetry, and Swift never mentions it. Fame might console a writer, but Swift dismisses fame in a short and brilliantly funny mock elegy. Poetic labors will be, like so much fattened poultry,

> Gone, to be never heard of more,
> Gone, where the *Chickens* went before.   (69–70)

The poet produces nothing anyone wants for either private or public life. The only way he can be useful, Swift implies, is by flattery or flunkyism. In a better world, the implication might be ironic. Certainly it reflects as much upon a corrupt society as upon the poet. Under the circumstances, poetry as poetry can do no good. The poet is an impotent observer in a decadent age.

In 1731, two years before Swift wrote "On Poetry," he gave the poet's figurative impotence a literal dimension. Insofar as he recognized humorously any of the old gods at all, he acknowledged Apollo as the ruler of poetic wits. He and Patrick Delany exchanged joking poems, during the 1720's, on Apollo's messages to the world below. In his letters Swift chalked up any lapses in poetic inspiration to neglect by Apollo. He was clearly thinking of Apollo as the god of poetry when he came to write "Apollo: Or, A Problem solved."

The poem begins with an accusation of poetic impotence that prefigures what is to come:

> *APOLLO,* God of Light and Wit,
> Could Verse inspire, but seldom writ: (1–2)

Swift proceeds to detail Apollo's abilities and advantages—his handsomeness, his skill at refining metals. As the catalogue progresses, Apollo more and more assumes the appearance of an effeminate fop:

> His Wig was made of sunny Rays,
> He crown'd his youthful Head with Bays:
> Not all the Court of Heav'n could shew
> So nice and so compleat a Beau.   (7–10)

With all his advantages, Apollo has a problem. He is unlucky in love. Swift assigns three reasons for the god's bad luck, and the third rounds off this curious poem. Apollo has left the Muses virgin in spite of their constant company. His singing voice can reach to the highest notes, and

At last, the Point was fully clear'd;
In short; *Apollo* had no Beard.   (31–32)

Of course, the poem is a jeu d'esprit, but one with a serious side. A joke is something you're not sure you don't really mean. If the reader dismisses, as the primary meaning of the poem, the rather modern notion that the writing of poetry is effeminate, he is left with the suggestion that the poet himself may be impotent. His poetry may be pretty or it may have a potential for usefulness, but in this world it may have nothing whatsoever to do with action or reform. Interpreted in this way, "Apollo" reinforces the first stanzas of "On Poetry": the poet has little to offer.

With such a grave allegation against the poet, the reader might conclude, Swift has dissociated himself decisively from the writing of poetry. Even in "On Poetry," however, Swift often speaks with straightforward sympathy and hints that he feels a kinship with the poet. In some of the best lines in the poem, he calls the poet's attention to common contemporary faults:

Or oft when Epithets you link,
In gaping Lines to fill a Chink;
Like stepping Stones to save a Stride,
In Streets where Kennels are too wide:
Or like a Heel-piece to support
A Cripple with one Foot too short:
Or like a Bridge that joins a Marish
To Moorlands of a diff'rent Parish.   (167–74)

The similes continue, five in a row, illustrating the proper use of comparisons and demonstrating that he is genuinely interested in helping the poet and genuinely concerned about reforming poetry. But the real proof that he identifies himself with poets and seriously interests himself in the writing of good poetry is that he is expressing his contempt for poets in the course of writing a poem.

How could Swift censure the poet so grievously, especially in a poem, and a poem that betrays feelings of kinship with poets in general? Why did he write poetry if he believed that poetry, however indispensable in a better world, was unprofitable for himself and ineffectual in reforming others? One is tempted to fall back on Davis' arguments and conclude that Swift somehow managed to write poetry without considering himself a poet or taking poetry seriously. Another answer, however, may be reached by asking another question. Why did Swift write satire if he believed that satire was unprofitable for himself and ineffectual in reforming others?

Swift almost invariably associates satire with poetry. He was, after all, a satiric poet. He also associates the drawbacks of writing the two. He always believed that his *Tale of a Tub* alienated the pious Queen Anne and helped to block his preferment in England. He always suspected that the Queen saw his early poem "The Windsor Prophecy" (1711) and resented its slander of her friend, the Duchess of Somerset. In the later verses "The Author upon Himself," the Queen appears as a royal prude, and the Duchess as a murderous hag vowing vengeance for Swift's reproaches and instilling poison into the royal ears. The same poem describes the sin of wit as "no venial Crime" (9). In "Verses on the Death of Dr. Swift," the so-called impartial speaker says Swift might have risen like other men if he had " 'spar'd his Tongue and Pen' " (355). Swift obviously imputes his lack of advancement to his satire, often more specifically to his satiric poetry. Writing to John Barber about a rhyming clergyman, he says, "I told you, he was a Man of Genius, and the best Poet we have, and you know, that is a Trade wherein I have medled too much for my Quiet, as well as my Fortune" (*Corr.,* Vol. 5, p. 96). These remarks may serve as glosses on the catalogue of worldly disadvantages Swift thrusts at the poet in the verses "On Poetry." The poverty, the lack of advancement, the derision the poet endures, he has endured too, as a satiric poet. He identifies himself with the poet, and his plight with the poet's plight.

Surely the efficacy of satire, however, distinguishes it from poetry. Surely the satirist has much to offer the world, however futile the poet's labors may be. Swift has his doubts. The satirist, in his mind, is as impotent as the poet. Time and again, he repeats the same complaint in different metaphors: satire is a mirror in which beholders see everybody's face but their own, the world's posteriors are insensitive to the satiric rod, every man carries a racket to hit the satiric ball toward his neighbor, and so forth. Swift spent his whole career developing strategies to obviate this problem, and every new work in his canon represents a new and more complex attempt to reach the reader. From *The Battle of the Books,* where Swift relies on personal satire and outright name-calling, to the *Modest Proposal,* where he carefully solicits and then betrays the reader's loyalty, to "The Day of Judgement," where his strategies are more intricate than ever before, he wrestles with the reader's reluctance to acknowledge himself in the satire. That he never, or only very late, found a viable solution is proved by his continual gibing at the satirist's impotence and general ridiculousness. The gibing is important to the proper interpretation of most of the major works and some of the minor: to the interpretation of the excremental poems, of the *Meditation upon a Broom-stick,* of *Gulliver's Travels.*

Does Swift's ridicule of the satirist demonstrate a lack of commitment to satire? Of course not. Swift continues to write satire as if he were fully satisfied with his role. *Why* he continues to write satire is a vexed question and one that literary critics may never definitively answer. Perhaps the best solution lies in Juvenal's phrase "difficile est saturam non scribere": "it is difficult not to write satire." Whatever conclusion the critics may reach, however, it undoubtedly applies as well to Swift's role as poet. The two roles were identified in his mind. In the disadvantages of the one, he saw the disadvantages of the other, and he satirized himself for putting up with those disadvantages without abdicating his responsibility in either role.

As a poet, Swift claims the authority to satirize poets who write amiss: he will indicate a better course. In "On Poetry," heroic verse comes under implied attack, the elegy is briefly and gently ridiculed, and bad poets in general are reduced to absurdity in lines that deliberately echo *The Dunciad.* But his prime target in the verses "On Poetry" seems to be the political panegyric. This he recommends ironically to the aspiring poet as a means of advancement. The stanzas that contain the recommendation are particularly interesting because they at once point to the satiric direction he wishes poetry to take and reflect further reservations about satire. Swift is obviously promoting, in lieu of the political panegyric, the political satire. He hints, however, that satire is simply the inversion of panegyric, that both are on a level with regard to the truth:

A Prince the Moment he is crown'd,
Inherits ev'ry Virtue round,

. . .

As soon as you can hear his Knell,
This God on Earth turns *Devil* in Hell.
And lo, his Ministers of State,
Transform'd to Imps, his Levee wait.   (191–92, 205–08)

Surely, the reader might think, Swift has in mind the lampoon, and not the legitimate political satire, for in that case, the implications of the inversion would not be so troublesome. But Swift spins out his infernal metaphor with great gusto and takes the opportunity to cast satiric barbs at the excise tax and the South-Sea scheme. He is clearly in his own milieu and reveling in the prospect of treating kings and ministers as devils and imps. If any doubts remained, his "Libel on Dr. Delany and a Certain Great Lord" (1730) and his "Legion Club" would dispel them. The "Libel" compares the King to Satan and Carteret to a viceroy-devil. The "Legion Club" sets the Irish Parliament in a combination Bedlam-Hell and identifies Swift's enemies as lunatics and demons. He cannot appeal to objective truth to justify some of his satire. He seems almost to flaunt the similarity between satire and the lying panegyric. Perhaps he feels that satire gives the truer impression because the truth is bad to an extreme. Perhaps his doubts about satire are fundamental. The reader of Swift must learn to live with mystery.

At any rate, Swift provides an exemplary alternative to the political panegyric—"On Poetry" itself. The end of the poem dramatizes his advice to the poet about the flattery of kings and courts. He pretends to eulogize the royal family and the ministry, but the panegyric recoils on the objects of praise. He allows scarcely any lapse into straightforward invective. The point is carried by the excess of the praise. And yet the praise is almost indistinguishable from that loyally offered up to the court by Eusden and Cibber. Queen Caroline apparently found it plausible enough to swallow it whole. Her advisers had to point out to her that the writer did not deserve a royal reward. Her feelings when she faced the truth at last can only be conjectured, but they surely proved to Swift the efficiency of this particular mode of satire, this way of overcoming the obstacle embodied in the phrase "*SATYR is a sort of* Glass . . ." In order to realize that a seeming panegyric is only mockery in disguise, one must first acknowledge that he lacks the virtues the poem describes. The Queen could not have derived Swift's real sentiments from passages of outright ridicule, because they don't exist. The only way she could have confronted the poem as a satire is by admitting to herself her own defects. Her advisers must have been uncommonly brave.

In a sense almost all Swift's verse is as much a critique of poetry as "On Poetry: A Rapsody." His poems to women—Stella, Vanessa, Lady Acheson—demonstrate by contrast the fatuity of contemporary love verse. The honest "Description of the Morning" and "Description of a City Shower" give the lie to the Neo-Virgilians. The excremental poems ridicule poetic love cant and pastoral conventions. In all his implicit recommendations to poets, the common denominator seems to be common sense. The old conventions are inapplicable to real life and offensive to the sensible man.

In the several poems primarily about poetry, the recommendation is explicit. "Directions for a Birth-day Song" (1729) makes a plea not so much for truth as for simple plausibility. Swift recognizes here, as in the verses "On Poetry," that satire can be as deceptive as encomium. Whereas the satirist, he says, blackens what before was white,

> Your Int'rest lyes to learn the knack
> Of whitening what before was black.   (115–16)

But satire, at least, will not draw in "twenty Gods of Rome or Greece" (2) whose exploits have no relation to the object of praise. If they did bear any relation, Swift says mischievously, the application would be scandalous:

> Why then appoint him Son of Jove,
> Who met his Mother in a grove;
> To this we freely shall consent,
> Well knowing what the Poets meant:
> And in their Sense, 'twixt me and you,
> It may be literally true.   (15–20)

The blunt man of sense—and Swift assumes this pose—would see exactly where his analogies were taking him.

Though Mary Barber, and not Swift, may have written "Apollo's Edict" (1721), she was too much his protégé not to have retailed his opinions.[1] The poem provides a convenient list of the improbable clichés he hated, and it reinforces the point that what he wanted was a fresher and simpler and more sensible kind of poetry. The verses "To Stella, Who Collected and Transcribed his Poems" show the same preoccupations. They focus, in particular, on the gross disparity between the cant and the real:

> Or should a Porter make Enquiries
> For *Chloe, Sylvia, Phillis, Iris*;
> Be told the Lodging, Lane, and Sign,
> The Bow'rs that hold those Nymphs divine;
> Fair *Chloe* would perhaps be found
> With Footmen tippling under Ground,   (39–44)

One cannot expect truth in this imperfect world, but one can demand a reasonable facsimile.

Next to poetry that lies in a palpable and glaring fashion, Swift hates the kind of poetry that sounds pretty and means nothing. The vogue for opera certainly helped to mold his point of view. Like most of his fellow writers, he despised it. Writing to Ambrose Philips in March 1708/9, he says, "The Town is run mad after a new Opera. Poetry and good Sense are dwindling like Echo into Repetition and Voice" (*Corr.,* Vol. 1, p. 129). The end of "Directions for a Birth-day Song" contains a glancing blow at Handel, not only a musician but George II's favorite composer and another damned German. The mockery of Handel follows an appropriate bit of ironic eulogy. Swift hails Queen Caroline for the lilting liquid sweetness of her name. The eulogy goes on and on—a full twenty lines of unremitting praise—until the reader begins to wonder whether Swift has a fetish for *r*'s and *l*'s. He is only emphasizing that the Queen's name, not her person or character, is the significant factor to the empty-headed poet. Perhaps, as it figures in panegyric, it is the significant factor to the empty-headed Queen as well. She presumably welcomes the eulogies that rely on the sound of her name.

The end of "Directions for a Birth-day Song" accomplishes several satiric hits at once. It mocks the poet's preference for sound by reaffirming the importance of sense. It reminds the Queen of the basic fact of death, a fact that no number of pretty panegyrics can ever obliterate. It explodes the poet's claim to confer immortality, at least when the candidate for eternal fame is only a word.

> What tho the royal Carcase must
> Squeez'd in a Coffin turn to dust;
> Those Elements her name compose,
> Like Atoms are exempt from blows.   (235-38)

The suggestion of a pun—the use of "name" instead of "good name"—completes the thrust at mistaken values. A "good name" might really immortalize the Queen and make the poet's lines live forever too.

Like "Directions for a Birth-day Song," the poem "A Love Song. In the Modern Taste" (1733) seems for a moment to leave open the question of where Swift stands. The point of the poem is the vacuity of modern love verse. The personification is laughable, the alliteration is without significance, and the classical allusion is empty. Nonetheless, the poem is curiously pretty:

> Thus when *Philomela* drooping,
>   Softly seeks her silent Mate;
> See the Bird of *Juno* stooping.
>   Melody resigns to Fate.   (29-32)

The appeal of the poem may be a trick of the Post-Keatsian ear, but Swift could also be following Pope in the parody of verses he has a latent fondness for. "A Love Song" recalls passages from Pope where he uses and parodies the pastoral at the same time. Maurice Johnson has even claimed that Pope may have had a hand in its composition.[2] Despite the prettiness, Swift is making fun of the precedence of sound over sense. The stupid valuing of music over meaning, he says most pointedly in the "Cantata," results in such nonsense as

Bo peep, bo peep, bo peep,
          bo peep, peep, bo bo peep.

Handel, the writers of opera, the silly "Namby Pamby" Philips, and the poets of modern love and birthday songs are all implicated in this single line.

Both implicitly and explicitly, Swift expresses his opinions about all kinds of verse—the heroic, the amatory, the elegiac, the panegyric, the senselessly bad. With such pronounced opinions and so little hesitancy in voicing them, he must have felt he had some expertise in the field. In this respect the letters hold some cruxes for critics, for they contain statements that seem to contradict one another. On the one hand, Swift can dismiss several of his best-known works as trifling: he passes off "Cadenus and Vanessa" (1713) as "only a cavalier business" (*Corr.,* Vol. 3, p. 130) and the Market Hill poems as "only amusements in hours of sickness or leisure" (Vol. 4, p. 27). He has good reason for playing down the importance of the poem for Vanessa after the sorry affair has ended, but he should have no such reservations about the popularity of "Death and Daphne" (1730) and "The Grand Question debated." Still, at times, he will extend his denigration of these private poems to cover his poetry as a whole. Writing to Pope and Bolingbroke in 1738, he says, "I have absolutely done with Poetry for several years past, and even at my best times I could produce nothing but trifles: . . ." (Vol. 5, p. 119). Such statements have given critics the impression that Swift did not profess to be a poet. Such statements, however, conflict with his sometimes enthusiastic, and even vainglorious, appreciation for his own poetry. Perhaps we can attribute the slighting remarks to his consciousness of the tradition he followed—the tradition of Butler and the seventeenth-century popular verse satirists. In the light of that tradition to take poetry too seriously would be a lapse in taste.

Swift's correspondence indicates that he did, in fact, think of himself as a poet; that he even indulged, with Prior and Pope, in little contests over poetic fame; that he wrote and rewrote with great earnestness and care, not merely "as a gentleman writes, to amuse himself and his friends";[3] that he worried about the flagging of his poetic abilities; that his friends thought of him as a poet and flattered him by saying so; that would-be poets came to him for advice; and that he gave the advice they asked for without any consciousness that he was meddling in an alien world.

Before Stella, his most intimate friend, Swift does not try to conceal the interest he has in his poems. With her he has no reason to pretend, and so the *Journal* provides an accurate record of his poetic enthusiasm. A case in point is his demeanor on the publication of his "Description of a City Shower." He likes the poem himself: "They say 'tis the best thing I ever writ," he says to Stella, "and I think so too."[4] His own affection for the poem helps to explain his almost fatherly concern for its reputation—his frequent inquiries to Stella about how it passes in Ireland and his evident pleasure in the good opinion of his fellow poets: "Mr. Rowe the poet desired me to dine with him to-day. I went to his office . . . and there was Mr. Prior; and they both fell commending my *Shower* beyond any thing that has been written of the kind: there never was such a Shower since Danaë's, &c. You must tell me how 'tis liked among you" (*Journal,* Vol. 1, p. 74). When he finds an Irishman who compliments the poem less warmly than it deserves, he imputes the coldness to the stupidity of the Irish: "Mr. Dopping I have seen, and he tells me coldly, my *Shower* is liked well enough; there's your Irish judgment" (p. 79). In this instance, as in many of Swift's comments about his poems, he is humorously exaggerating his concern and his annoyance at lukewarm readers. The concern and annoyance are not less real for being disguised as a joke.

He must have wanted very much to be popular in his own country. His fear that "City Shower" was not being acclaimed in Ireland recurs again and again: "Could you have guessed the *Shower in Town* to be mine? How chance you did not see that before your last letter went; but I suppose you in Ireland did not think it worth mentioning" (p. 86). Stella apparently attempts to reassure Swift that the poem is liked, but the reassurance is not adequate for him: "My *Shower* admired with YOU; why, the bishop of Clogher says, he has seen something of mine of the same sort, better than the *Shower.* I suppose he means *The Morning;* but it is not half so good. . . . How does MD like it? and do they taste it *all*? &c." (p. 109). Stella seems to have accused him of not wanting the approval of the Irish. He denies it but hints, again, that the Irish are stupid: "I suppose you think it is a piece of affectation in

me to wish your Irish folks would not like my *Shower;* but you
are mistaken. I should be glad to have the general applause there as
I have it here (though I say it) but I have only that of one or two,
and therefore I would have none at all, but let you all be in the
wrong" (p. 127). Again, the joke has a serious side: Swift's pride
in the poem was real.

The progress of "City Shower" through the *Journal to Stella*
has parallels in the records of other poems. Swift shows a similar
concern about the fates of "The Windsor Prophecy" ("I like it
mightily; I don't know how it will pass" Vol. 2, p. 444), and "The
Fable of Midas" (1712) ("tell me how it passes with you" p. 488).
Such concern is not customary in a writer only of trifles. Swift was
seriously interested in writing good poems. That his ambition for
success in the endeavor persisted throughout his later life is proved
by his complaints about a decline in poetic facility. Old age seems
to mean for him first a loss of health and second an increasing difficulty in finding a rhyme. When he laments the decline of "invention," he almost always associates it not with his prose but with
his poetry. Apparently, he assumes that his prose will take care of
itself, but he worries tremendously that old age will strip him of
his poetic powers. His letters to Pope are full of comments like
this: "My poetical fountain is drained, and I profess I grow
gradually so dry, that a Rhime with me is almost as hard to find
as a Guinea . . ." (*Corr.,* Vol. 4, p. 31). Again, such concern is not
customary in a writer only of trifles. Sometimes Swift brags of the
ease with which he writes, as if the product were negligible. But
once in a while he reveals the extent of his labors. Writing to
Charles Ford in reference to "The Bubble" (1720), he talks about
the pains he has taken to make it completely correct. Swift did
much trifling in his life, but some of his poems he wanted to be
first-rate.

He may not have believed he was as good a poet as Pope or
Prior, but he certainly believed they were all working along the
same lines. With regard to Pope, this belief takes the form of a few
joking references to a poetical contest. In 1725, for example, Swift
writes to Pope, "I am so full (quod ad me attinet) of grand designs
that I believe I shall never bring them to pass but to your Comfort
(grandia loquimur) they are all in prose" (Vol. 3, pp. 78–79).
With regard to Prior, the contest occupies a large number of entries

in the *Journal to Stella.* Swift evidently found the poet's company
both flattering and fun. They passed the time together making light
of each other's verses, Swift reading Prior aloud in a deliberately
pedestrian way and Prior retaliating by making Swift sound just as
flat (*Journal,* Vol. 1, pp. 145–46).

Prior must have been at the time and in Swift's circle the poet
par excellence of light verse, for Swift seems to feel that no one
could outdo him, except perhaps himself. In reference to the verses
on "The Virtues of Sid Hamet the Magician's Rod" (1710), he
writes, "Hardly any body suspects me for them, only they think
no-body but Prior or I could write them" (p. 65). Lord Peterborough and Robert Harley manipulated both contestants with
sly skill. Swift records an instance when Peterborough fought off
rivals for the privilege of reading "Sid Hamet" aloud, and while he
read the supposedly anonymous poem, Harley kept nudging Swift
to take notice of the beauties. Prior humorously accused Peterborough of being the author, Peterborough accused Prior, Prior
then turned the compliment to Swift, and Swift returned it to
Prior (p. 60). On another occasion, Harley seemed to decide the
general contest in favor of Swift by saying that one of his poems
was the best he ever read (p. 92). Swift must have realized that
this was a spurious victory, for he was afterward content to share
the laurels: "Lewis went away, and Prior and I sat on, where we
complimented one another for an hour or two upon our mutual
wit and poetry" (p. 98).

At the time of these entries, in 1710, Prior was an established
poet, having already written many of his famous social poems and
the lengthy *Solomon.* In Prior, Swift was taking on a formidable,
if playful, opponent. His boldness in daring to compare himself
with Prior marks the reality of his ambition. Only a man who
wanted to be a poet and believed himself capable of poetry would
have run the risks of competing, however lightheartedly, with Prior
and Pope.

Swift's friends never doubted that he was capable of good
poetry. Prior thought him worthy of competition, and he writes,
with an enclosure of his verses, "Sic est, homo sum, and am not
ashamed to send those very Verses to One who can make much
better" (*Corr.,* Vol. 2, p. 328). Pope asks continually about the
progress of Swift's poems, and he valued them enough to publish

in joint volumes. Bolingbroke, writing to Swift, casually classifies him as a poet (Vol. 3, p. 349). Erasmus Lewis worries about Swift's finances, he says, because versemen are notoriously naive about business affairs (p. 508). More than his other friends, Lord Bathurst overwhelms Swift with praise of his poetry. He recommends that Swift drink woman's milk to allay his feverish spirits, which would otherwise break out and cause a general conflagration. He accuses the poet of turning the brains of poor innocent people (pp. 454–55). He compares him, rather coyly, with the poetic giants of the past: "have not y^u stoln the sweetness of y^r Numbers from Dryden & Waller, have not y^u borrow'd thoughts from Virgil & Horace, at least I am sure I have seen something like them in those Books . . ." (p. 407). Swift must have found these tributes gratifying, but friends are partial. The real proof that he was a poet in his own time comes from men less close to him—from the anonymous correspondent, for example, who writes to him as the "king of poets" (Vol. 4, p. 289). Not only did Swift consider himself a poet, but he had from others support for his point of view.

His reputation as a poet ensured his reputation as a critic of poetry, and aspiring unknowns applied to him to suggest themes and correct their lines. One young aspirant says he will not venture into print without the advice of an established poet like him (p. 278). Not all the applicants were unknowns: Pope encourages Swift to propose corrections and says he will lay his poems by until his friend comes to carp at them (p. 148). These appeals, and others like them, provide another measure of Swift's contemporary success as a poet. He actually replied to some of these applicants and thereby showed that he believed himself competent at the role they assigned him.

In the course of these replies, his familiar comments on Dryden's triplets, on Thomson's descriptive verse, and on Pope's "bad" rhymes and triplets show his interest in the theory and practice of poetry. Other remarks, less well-known, offer insight into what he expected good poetry to accomplish. Swift wanted poetry to be accessible to the common reader. His concern for the reader of "middling" intelligence might have resulted from his long struggle to reach and reform all the readers of satire. It might have reflected his own wide base of popularity. Whatever the reason for it, his emphasis on the many distinguished him from some of his fellow poets, whose emphasis was on the few.

Pope, for example, writes to Swift in 1731, "whenever you see what I am now writing, you'll be convinced I would please but a few . . ." (Vol. 3, p. 510). Swift ignores Pope's predilection and counsels him continually to observe the profit and pleasure of a wider audience. With regard to the *Dunciad Variorum,* he cautions Pope to be ample in his notes for the sake of the provincial reader, "for I have long observed that twenty miles from London no body understands hints, initial letters, or town-facts and passages . . ." (p. 293). With regard to the epitaph Pope composed for Gay, Swift suggests several changes so it will be "clearer to common readers" (Vol. 4, p. 133). The "Epistle to Bathurst" would be faultless, he says, "but that some parts of it are not so obvious to midling Readers" (pp. 134-35). And Pope was not the only offender. Swift warns Thomas Tickell that all his readers will not be so sagacious as Swift himself: "I see what *this* and *that* refer too, but in the line just before there are two words, *present* and *past* and in the next line above *virtues* and *boast,* which will make some difficulty to a common reader" (Vol. 3, p. 481). Comments like these demonstrate that Swift was confident in his role as poetic adviser, but more than that, they point in the direction his own poetry will take. For he was no literary elitist. In lines that are clear and simple and seemingly bare of poetic device, in lines that present no apparent stumbling blocks for the "common reader," he embeds his complex rhetorical strategies.

He was a conscious critic of poetry and a conscious poet as well. At times, he may seem harshly critical of poets, but his satire is self-directed, an indication of involvement in the poet's thankless task. At times, he may seem to tear at the foundations of poetry— rending to shreds the heroic, the panegyric, and the amatory. Actually, he is either censuring the contemporary abuses of these styles or ridiculing their least sensible elements. Never is he assailing poetry itself. His literary criticism, whether in his letters or in his poems, demonstrates his fears about the progress of poetry in his time and his desire for reform.

To the reader who likes eighteenth-century poetry in general, the reformer Swift may recall Jack in *A Tale of a Tub,* who destroyed his father's coat by stripping off the decorations. But on a closer view, he more resembles Martin, with his coat finally reduced to a state of innocence. He reforms without really disturbing the essentials. His poetry moves in a healthy direction—in the direction of simplicity, clarity, and concern for the common reader.

3. The Odes

Swift was not always a maverick in poetry. This rebel began as an idolator of the modes and methods of others, and by doing so betrayed his own best instincts and played false with his personality, his most powerful instrument of persuasion. The poems he produced during his early period were consistently bad. A few critics, Yeats for one, have found material to admire even in the odes, but the poems interest most readers only as a great man's juvenilia. Apart from their historical value, however, the early odes compel our attention by signaling the presence of latent satiric genius. What I want to explore here, besides the place of these poems in Swift's personal and poetic development and the disappointing discrepancies between them and his mature works, are the reassuring lapses into something like satire.

Common themes bind the odes together. In each of the poems, Swift tries to define and distinguish goodness and greatness, to separate reality and illusion, to exalt the few at the expense of the many. With the common themes come common images. Flies and gnats buzz around wit and excellence. The sun dispels the vapors. The deluge recedes and advances. The storm abates and increases in violence. The garden appears a paradise and a promise of future good. The Goths pour from the north in swarms. Recurrent images are couched in recurrent words, and phrases from one ode reappear in another. The poet's pompous conception of himself is consistent in all. The most obvious tie, however, is genre: all but the last two are written in the Pindaric manner as it was conceived in the seventeenth century.

In his life of Cowley, Samuel Johnson describes the spread of Pindarism: "all the boys and girls caught the pleasing fashion, and they that could do nothing else could write like Pindar."[1] It so happened that all the boys and girls were wasting their time, for the irregularity they admired in Pindar and tried to reproduce was nothing more than a misreading of Greek metrics. Johnson probably has in mind this basic mistake when he writes that the mode of composition was "erroneous,"[2] but he is surely judging the miserable results as much as the original error. Swift was among those who caught the pleasing fashion, and the mode of composition was especially erroneous for him. In the interest of the genre he suppressed his comic genius. He was never to write any other pieces so devoid of irony and humor.

The Pindaric tradition required from the poet irregularity, grandeur, and obscurity. Cowley's "contributions" to the genre were the metaphysical cast of his wit, a quality that interfered with grandeur in the true Pindaric sense, and the feebleness of his diction. But who, after all, could have done better? Dryden produced several great odes, but he also wrote a few emphatic failures. He frequently lapsed into self-parody in the course of an ode, as if he realized the limitations of the style. Such doubtful achievements prepared the way for Swift's first venture into poetry.

He labored hard to fulfill the misconceived requirements of the genre. His lines are sometimes so irregular that the reader cannot say them aloud without pausing awkwardly or slurring words together. A few lines from his "Ode to the King. On his Irish Expedition. And The Success of his Arms in general" (1690–1) illustrate the difficulties:

> And what I us'd to laugh at in *Romance,*
> And thought too great ev'n for effects of Chance,   (62–63)

In some a parenthesis creates an awkward hiatus:

> Our *Prince* has charm'd its many hundred Eyes;

Has lull'd the Monster in a Deep
And (I hope) an Eternal Sleep,   (78–80)

The passage reads well as parody.

The same poem, though not the most obscure of the odes, is obscure enough to satisfy the most enthusiastic. Swift writes a whole stanza about James II without identifying him by name. The only clues to the subject of the stanza are the phrase "Your fond *Enemy*" (101) and the vague biographical facts of the description. The reader who confuses James with the subject of the next stanza, Louis XIV, commits a pardonable error. Swift, perhaps realizing how difficult his poetry could be, studs his early odes with footnotes; yet many almost incomprehensible lines, like certain passages from the "Ode to the Athenian Society" (1692) he leaves unannotated. His indulgence is syntactic mysteries, like these from the same poem, hardly helps the situation:

Else why should the fam'd *Lydian* King,
Whom all the *Charms* of an Usurped Wife and State,
With all that Power unfelt, courts Mankind to be Great,
    Did with new, unexperienc't Glories wait,
Still wear, still doat on his *Invisible Ring*.   (153–57)

He could have spared the reader this kind of muddle, but he gloried in his obscurity. He took it as evidence of kinship with his models. Writing to his cousin, Thomas Swift, in 1692, he says: "but igad I can not write anything easy to be understood thô it were but in praise of an old Shooo" (*Corr.,* Vol. 1, p. 10). He may have associated obscurity with grandeur, the third of the Pindaric requirements. The whole tenor of his poems shows his eagerness for epic dignity. Especially telling is the kind of writer (Homer, Virgil, Milton, Dryden) he chooses to imitate.

In his later life Swift prided himself on his originality. His advertisement to *Poems,* 1735, shows that he intended not to borrow from other authors at all, whether from the common store of old poetic conventions or from the fairly fresh thoughts of contemporary writers: *"the Author never was known either in Verse or Prose to borrow any Thought, Simile, Epithet, or particular Manner of Style; but whatever he writ, whether good, bad, or indifferent, is an Original in itself.*"[3] Ironically, he anticipated these sentiments in 1693, in the ode "To Mr. Congreve." Quoting from an earlier poem, lost since his time, he thus advises Congreve:

> *Beat not the dirty paths where vulgar feet have trod,*
> *But give the vigorous fancy room.*   (205–06)

By 1693 he had betrayed his notion of originality time and again in the only poems he had as yet attempted.

Naturally, Cowley provided Swift with an extraordinary number of hints. In his *Letter Concerning the Sacramental Test*, Swift quotes from his predecessor's love lyrics and says he found them remarkable even at the age of fifteen.[4] In 1692 he wrote to Thomas Swift, "I find when I writt what pleases me I am Cowley to my self and can read it a hundred times over" (*Corr.*, Vol. 1, p. 9). He clearly thought Cowley the best of models, and the degree to which the odes depend on Cowley's poetry testifies to this admiration. The "Ode to the Athenian Society" is an obvious reply to Cowley's "Ode to the Royal Society." The Platonism in the first and the assertion of faith—"I believe in much, I ne're can hope to see" (134)—answer the scientific skepticism in the second. Ehrenpreis finds not only general parallels to Cowley but also echoes of him in the details of the odes, especially in the "Ode to the King," the "Ode to the Honourable Sir William Temple" (1692), and the ode "To Mr. Congreve."[5] In all of the odes, Cowley's example is ever present to Swift's mind.

The heroic poets, too, served as models. The references to Homer and Virgil, though few, are distinct enough to provide an index to the kind of heroic poet Swift aspired to be. Stanza IV of the "Ode to the King" contains several Homeric allusions: a dark cloud hides a destroying angel from the poet's sight, an angel who takes up a stand between King William and fate and deflects the "flying Deaths" with his "everlasting Shield." Stanza III of the "Ode to the Athenian Society" refers to a Virgilian cloud—the one that hid Aeneas when he entered Carthage. Echoes of Milton abound in the "Ode to Dr. William Sancroft, Late Lord Archbishop of Canterbury" (1692). The Miltonic diction of the opening lines is unmistakable:

TRUTH is eternal, and the Son of Heav'n,
>   Bright effluence of th' immortal ray,   (1–2)

The resemblance to Milton's "Bright effluence of bright essence increate" is almost obtrusive. Ehrenpreis finds some instances of Miltonic allusion a little more subtle than this. The lines on sublunary "wild and imperfect" shapes in stanza II resemble Milton's lines on fancy's "Wild work" in "misjoining shapes" in Book V of *Paradise Lost*. Milton's sun in Book III sheds its "gentle penetration, though unseen." Swift's Sancroft, like a star, sheds his "sacred influence," "tho' all unseen" (153).[6]

The poet's use of Dryden in the "Ode to the King" is significant and surprising in light of the constant malevolence toward Dryden that critics have always attributed to him. Malevolent or not, he derived his description of the Scots from Dryden's picture of the English in *Absalom and Achitophel*. The Scots—"that Discontented Brood" (82)—assert their "Titles to be *Jews*" (85). The general parallel to Dryden's "Headstrong, Moody, Murmuring race" is strongly suggestive. The resemblance of line 89 ("And one would think 'twere past Omnipotence to please") is too close for coincidence to Dryden's line 48 ("No King could govern, nor no God could please").[7]

But Swift's models were not all heroic. George Mayhew finds the influence of Shakespeare and Donne pervasive in the early odes. According to Mayhew, the poems written between 1689 and 1691 reflect the reading of *Love's Labour's Lost, A Midsummer Night's Dream, The Comedy of Errors*, and the histories, especially the *Henry* plays. Early in 1692, Donne began to prevail among his models, and Mayhew identifies lines from the "Ode to the Athenian Society" which closely resemble lines from the *Songs and Sonets*.[8] The Spenserian romance completes the Homeric catalogue of derivations. Swift several times mentions the romance in the odes, usually to scoff at it, but stanza III of the "Ode to the King" may owe something to its influence:

And thus He did the Airy Goddess Court,
>   He sought Her out in Fight,
>   And like a Bold Romantick Knight

Rescu'd Her from the Giant's Fort:
The Tyrant Death lay crouching down,   (35–39)

Pindar, Cowley, Homer, Virgil, Milton, Dryden, Shakespeare, Donne, Spenser—Swift's debts are staggering and provoke the question, What in the odes is his own? The answer must be not much, and that is one reason why they are so bad. Only the greatest poets can borrow so much from other writers without betraying their own inadequacy, or at least their sense of it. Later in life Swift borrows too, but his uses of convention are more in keeping with his comic genius. The first line of "A Description of the Morning" is heavy with alliteration: "NOW hardly here and there an Hackney-Coach . . ." Its context transforms it into something fresh and exciting, as it signals the witty ordering of city imagery in the surprisingly apt pattern of the old pastoral verse.

Many other such transformations could be cited, but among the early instances "The Story of Baucis and Philemon. Ov. Met. 1.8." is the most sustained and most successful. Written in 1706 and revised in 1708–9, fifteen years after the last ode, it turns the Ovidian myth into a boistrous exercise in debunking, with the poet in a carnival mood thumbing his nose at myth, modern life, parsonhood, and sentimentality. In the *Metamorphoses* pious old Baucis and Philemon, exactly the same age and married from their youth, have lived through all the stages of life as equal partners and sharers of their modest cottage. When the gods Jupiter and Mercury, disguised as mortals, come to call on the community, only they will admit and entertain them. They feed the gods a homely meal, though mouthwatering in the long description. Jupiter and Mercury then invite them to observe the punishment of their neighbors for the sin of impiety, and the two duly lament the fate of the innundated sinners. While they weep, their own home becomes a magnificent temple, marble columns taking the place of forked wooden supports, and thatch turning into yellow gold. The gods invite them to choose yet another reward. The old people, devoted both to the gods and to each other, ask that they become priests of the temple and that they die at the same hour. At the moment of death they are transformed into trees, which the Ovidian narrator says he has seen and decorated himself.

Not so in Swift. In his verses, the gods are demoted to saints, and they are disguised, more specifically, as canting strollers, beggars who try to wheedle and whine their way into neighborhood homes. In the earlier version of the poem, before Swift showed it to Addison, the kind of confidence game they play is illustrated:

> They call'd at ev'ry Dore; Good People,
> My Comrade's Blind, and I'm a Creeple   (15–16)

The pious old man and woman, who are not only simple but a bit simple-minded, at first take the miracle of the replenished jug as a sign that the visitors might be diabolic. (In the earlier version the jug is full of unpoetic beer.) Neither they nor the saints show any pity for the unfortunate neighbors, whom the visitors rather vindictively drown:

> But for that Pack of churlish Boors
> Not fitt to live on Christian Ground,
> They and their Village shall be droun'd,   (1706, 86–88)

Without asking Baucis and Philemon what they prefer, the saints change their cottage into a church. The metamorphoses are more grotesque than splendid, as the heavy wall clambers upward, and the chair crawls along it like a huge snail. Metaphysical wit creeps in as the kettle hangs upside down, with "It's Inclination for below" (1706, 100), and turns into a bell. Far from being a magnificent temple, the church is emphatically rural, with posted ballads becoming churchly ensigns familiar to country parishes. In Swift the changes are complexly mechanical, and the idea of spiritual metamorphosis is lost.

The same is true of the changes in the couple. Rather than asking to die at the same hour as Baucis, Philemon has a greedy request:

> *Philemon,* having paus'd a while,
> Return'd 'em Thanks in homely Stile;
> Then said; my House is grown so Fine,
> Methinks, I still wou'd call it mine:
> I'm Old, and fain wou'd live at Ease,
> Make me the *Parson,* if you please.   (1708–9, 111–16)

The joke is that he becomes a bad person, negligent in his duty, since his transformation is merely a change in external appearance. The further joke is that most parsons are just like him. His wife is equally unaffected in a spiritual sense, but likes wearing better clothes and being called "Madam." Though they have not requested to die at the same time, they do turn into trees. As Philemon begins to sprout, Swift jests with the idea of cuckoldry. For the Ovidian old man who attests to the truth of the story, the poet substitutes the tiresome Goodman Dobson:

> Remembers he the Trees has seen;
> He'll talk of them from Noon till Night,
> And goes with Folks to shew the Sight: (1708–9, 166–68)

The point of the metamorphosis disappears: First, the couple is changed only outwardly, and their second transformation into trees does not ensure their lasting love. The parsons who succeed them precipitate the unpoetic end:

> Till once, a Parson of our Town,
> To mend his Barn, cut *Baucis* down;
> At which, 'tis hard to be believ'd,
> How much the other Tree was griev'd,
> Grew Scrubby, dy'd a-top, was stunted:
> So, the next Parson stub'd and burnt it.   (1708–9, 173–78)

The eternity of love, the piety of priesthood, and the poetry of metamorphosis turn to bathos in this anticlimax. At the same time that poetry is dying, reality is coming to the fore. Barns need building, trees are trees, and no concession can be made to sentimental myth.

Scholars are beginning to realize that Ovid's tale is touched with a humor and cynicism that would have pleased Swift. The story probably came to him, however, through such renditions as Dryden's, which is unremittingly grandiose.

Swift did not always choose to debunk conventions, as he does here. Sometimes, as in the Stella poems, he relies on small but important changes in the tradition. The point is that he was not afraid of altering the mode either radically or subtly, for he trusted his own creative talent. That confidence is missing from the odes, where the borrowings appear as obtrusive signs of homage to poets he admired.

We can only speculate about what Swift's odes might have been if he had allowed his natural inclinations free rein. Certainly the good passages are those which point forward to his later satiric style, not those which point backward to his antecedents. The derivative passages are too palpably derivative, and sometimes hackneyed as well. He does not scruple to draw upon the tritest figures in the common poetic store. Achilles' heel appears in the "Ode to the King." In the "Ode to the Athenian Society," Swift makes much of the Nile's origin. In the ode to Congreve, he pictures himself as a victorious wren perched on an eagle's wing. These figures are the kind that provokes his and Mrs. Barber's scorn in "Apollo's Edict" about thirty years later:

> No Simile shall be begun,
> With *rising* or with *setting* Sun:
> And let the *secret Head of* Nile
> Be ever banish'd from your Isle.
>
> . . .
>
> The *Bird of Jove* shall toil no more,
> To teach the humble *Wren* to soar.   (12–15, 25–26)

"Apollo's Edict" reads like a bitter commentary on the early odes, from a man who was expiating his own youthful sins by castigating trite and borrowed phrases.

Swift's borrowings, however crude and misconceived, at least guide us to his conception of himself in the 1690's. The writers he chose to imitate prove that he wanted to be a heroic poet. His use of the old poetic conceits shows that he thought of himself as a traditional writer, not as the poetic rebel he was to become. The odes show that for the young Swift poetry was a conventionally divine calling. In the ode "Occasioned by Sir William Temple's late Illness and Recovery" (1693), he speaks of a poetic priesthood and includes himself among the initiated:

> Unknown the forms we the high-priesthood use
> At the divine appearance of the Muse,
> Which to divulge might shake profane belief,
> And tell the irreligion of my grief: (75–78)

In the "Ode to Sir William Temple," he says he owes his vocation to Nature's decree, that she has tied him to the muse's oars. And like Pope after him, he claims that he cannot help himself:

> Whate'er I plant (like Corn on Barren Earth)
>   By an equivocal Birth
>   Seeds and runs up to Poetry.   (210–12)

Both the divinity and the inevitability of the poetic calling he was to mock in later life.

As a mature poet he could see the adolescent element in his early idea of himself. At least, he could see it in others. He ridicules Cassinus and Peter in 1731 for their rapturous conferences on "Love and Books" (4), though the same sophomoric blend of philosophy and love captured the young poet's fancy in the "Ode to the Athenian Society" (55–56). Love in the odes is always betraying the author's youth, always intruding into the sober discussions of other subjects. In the "Ode to the King" death comes, like love, wrapped in fire and makes every breast its home (68–70). Love in the odes, though always adolescent, is not always so idealistic. Ehrenpreis has noticed that Swift's sexual interests crop up time and again in these early poems.[9] The ode to Congreve, in particular, shows that his preoccupation with sex could reveal itself in the most unlikely places. The notion of poetry as a divine calling, the Platonistic point of view, the hero-worship he indulges in, the coupling of philosophy and love, death and love, poetry and love—all show his immaturity. He ridicules most of these attitudes in later life. Perhaps he revolted against the kind of poetry the odes represent because he rejected the kind of person he was when he wrote them. Perhaps, like most men, he tended to condemn what he associated with his adolescence. That the adolescent poems were failures must have intensified this impulse.

Swift wrote the poems in part to please Sir William Temple, and he probably took up some points of view that fit Temple better than himself. In some passages a personality more familiar to us seems to break through. Swift puns occasionally, makes covert jokes, and bursts into satiric invective. Usually at these points, when he begins to write like the Swift we know from the satires, the meter becomes more regular and the poetry more coherent.

Like Dryden, Swift could not always maintain the sobriety appropriate to the Pindaric poet. The poems are not really better for the lapses, but the lapses are frequently better than the rest of the poems.

Swift's punning in the odes links the early poems to the later satires. Punning was for him a kind of signature, and his first puns provide a slight sign of his latent comic talents. He plays in the "Ode to the Athenian Society" on "ebb and flow":

> AS when the *Deluge* first began to fall,
> That *mighty Ebb* never to flow again, (1–2)

In the "Ode to Sir William Temple" he puns on "golden" while describing the alchemic pretensions of philosophy:

> And we the bubbled Fools
> Spend all our present Stock in hopes of golden Rules. (26–27)

In the same poem he plays with the ideas of the gamester's "box" and the "box" as coffin for those slain in war:

> Fortune the Gamesters does beguile,
> Yet at the last the Box sweeps all away. (79–80)

The puns, not exactly rib-splitting, are less interesting in themselves than as signposts for the future. Swift, for example, makes almost the same pun on "golden" in the satiric "Epistle to a Lady" as in the "Ode to Sir William Temple" forty years before.

More substantial a link is the similarity of certain images in the odes to certain images in the satires. The lines describing the muse among the city beaux in the ode to Congreve resemble the picture of Gulliver among the Yahoos:

> *Sham'd and amaz'd, beholds the chatt'ring throng,*
> *To think what cattle she has got among;*
> *But with the odious smell and sight annoy'd,*
> *In haste she does th'offensive herd avoid.* (223–26)

Swift's obscene play with the idea of the French king's anal fistula in the "Ode to the King" resembles satiric passages on

Louis XIV in the "Digression on Madness."[10] The coupling of the
fistula and false greatness anticipates the whole argument of the
Discourse Concerning the Mechanical Operation of the Spirit. The
passage about Philosophy's varied dress in the "Ode to the
Athenian Society" is similar to the description of the embellished
coats in *A Tale of a Tub*. And the actions of the Puritans in the ode
to Sancroft resemble Jack's actions in the same prose satire:

> Say what their senseless malice meant,
>   To tear Religion's lovely face;
>   Strip her of ev'ry ornament and grace,
> In striving to wash off th'imaginary paint: (247–50)

Some images in the odes, then, connect directly with images in
the satires. Other images are generically satiric without having
specific correspondents in the later satires. The description of
James II in the "Ode to the King" gives proof of Swift's satiric
bent:

> His scrap of Life is but a Heap of Miseries,
>   The Remnant of a falling Snuff,
>   Which hardly wants another puff,
>   And needs must *stink* when e're it dies;   (107–10)

In the same poem the lines on Louis XIV as a "Gilded Meteor"
(122) point in the direction of satire:

> Stay but a little while and down again 'twill come,
>   And end as it began, in Vapour, Stink, and Scum.   (128–29)

The intense image of nausea in the "Ode to Sir William Temple"
anticipates Swift's strategic shocks in—to take a few examples—
the excremental poems, the chapters on Gulliver's visit to the
Academy, and the description of the Aeolists. Shock became for
him a primary rhetorical strategy, and the picture of the pedants
regurgitating their lessons takes its place in a long series of similar
images:

> And sick with Dregs of Knowledge grown,
>   Which greedily they swallow down,
> Still cast it up and nauseate Company.   (47–49)

In the odes he identifies his enemies with flies and gnats and worms and cattle, comparisons recalling the animal imagery in the later satires.

Finally, in the odes Swift presents his first full-blown satiric portrait.[11] The picture of the Farnham boy turned city beau in the ode to Congreve points to his later skill and his affinity with master portraitists like Pope. The odes probably encouraged Swift's tendency toward the startling, grotesque pictures and images that his later writing is famous for. Insofar as these pictures and images derived from experience with metaphysical poetry, he owed the tradition a degree of gratitude.

Though the satiric imagery of the odes continues into the later prose, the conception of satire is different. In the early verse references to satire are pompous and consistent with the generally pompous tone of the poems. If Swift conceives of the poet as a high priest, he conceives of the satirist as the scourge of God. Both notions will remind the reader of Pope—in the "Epilogue to the Satires," for example. Pope might have spoken these lines from the ode to Congreve, but they are uncharacteristic of the later Swift, except as he appears in his epitaph:

> My hate, whose lash just heaven has long decreed
> Shall on a day make sin and folly bleed;   (133–34)

Another passage from the same ode is not quite so difficult to reconcile with the views of the later poet:

> A pride that well suspends poor mortals fate,
> Gets between them and my resentment's weight,
> Stands in the gap 'twixt me and wretched men,
> T'avert th'impending judgments of my pen.   (45–48)

Here he is on the verge of articulating a dilemma perennial to the satirist—a dilemma that took on real force for him later. The satirist frequently claims that the objects of his satire are too trivial for hatred, and yet, in light of that pretense, how can he justify his satire? The dilemma is Swift's own, even later in life, but the tone, the supreme confidence in satire, is incongruous with his later views.

The early references to satire are almost triumphant. The later ones are fraught with self-doubt. He came to believe that the satirist might be impotent, his motives impure. Perhaps the change in Swift's attitude toward satire is consistent with the change in his idea of himself, and the two combine to alter the nature of his poetry. The early poet is doubt-free, the attitude toward satire is confident, and the verse is full of "poetic" bombast. The later Swift is doubt-ridden, the attitude toward satire is ambiguous, and the verse is determinedly antipoetic. Perhaps the acknowledgment of general human weakness which came with his maturity helped to transmute his poems. Certainly, his later conception of himself and of satire would preclude the writing of any poems like the odes. For the later Swift the early poems have far too many pretensions.

The last two odes he wrote show him turning in a new and more promising direction, for they are composed in the heroic couplet perfected by the Augustans and not in the Pindaric manner typical of Cowley. Even more promising is his farewell to his youthful style in "Sir William Temple's late Illness," the very last of the odes. Speaking to his muse, he says:

> There thy enchantment broke, and from this hour
> I here renounce thy visionary pow'r;
> And since thy essence on my breath depends,
> Thus with a puff the whole delusion ends.   (151–54)

He dismisses the muse of his odes because she has failed to provide him with the hope of success—probably in the eyes of Sir William Temple. A long silence of five years ensues, before Swift begins to write for himself rather than for his mentor. The new poems, beginning with "Verses wrote in a Lady's Ivory Table-Book," have none of the pomposity of the early odes. They are hardly "poetical" at all. His failure at the high-flown style of poetry fostered a life-long animus against it. Quite naturally, the man who wrote the early odes was to write, later in life, such poems as "On Poetry: A Rapsody."

4. The Two "Descriptions"

Just as critical skills developed in explicating Pope have hampered appreciation of Swift's poetry when wrongly applied to him, so critical knowledge of how classical allusion works in most eighteenth-century poetry has been misapplied to "A Description of the Morning" (1709) and "A Description of a City Shower" (1710). When Dryden or Pope refers to Homer or Virgil, he often means to imply that his modern heroes are villains or buffoons. The mock-heroic enjoyed such a vogue in the Augustan Age, and modern critics have become so comfortable with this subgenre, that they can now talk with some ease about the effects of a belittling classical reference. The temptation is to read Swift's mock-eclogue and his mock-georgic as if they worked precisely like a conventional mock-heroic poem, and therefore to infer that Swift hated London.

The argument depends upon the assumption that the figure standing behind the poems and pronouncing judgment on city life is none other than Virgil, a critic not lightly gainsaid. Steele's prefaces to the two poems, both published first in his *Tatler* papers, point in a rather different direction, and since the thrust of his remarks does not seem to have hit home, they deserve to be quoted again. The introduction to "A Description of the Morning" deals with certain "insects" who have been tormenting the town "for half an age" with "fantastical descriptions" and praises of

Phillis and Chloris, those perennial pastoral maidens.[1] Steele very specifically identifies Swift's intention: "to avoid their strain."[2] In doing so, Swift has "run into a way perfectly new, and described things exactly as they happen: he never forms fields, or nymphs, or groves, where they are not; but makes the incidents just as they really appear."[3] As Steele reads Swift, the poet is not urging any particular attitude toward fields and nymphs and groves where they *are* (in the land of Virgil, myth-encrusted by common consent). Swift's argument is with the imitators of Virgil, who impose their "fantastical" maunderings upon a here and now so insistently real that morning occurs "at this end of the town, where my kinsman at present lodges."[4] The introduction to "A Description of a City Shower" focuses on substantially the same issue—Steele's boredom with the contemporary abuse of classical material. He says that "whenever I find the winds begin to rise in a new heroic poem, I generally skip a leaf or two until I come into fair weather."[5] He explicitly exempts Virgil's showers from censure and reserves ridicule for modern imitators.[6]

No evidence exists to discredit Steele's readings—if indeed they are his and not Swift's. He was certainly in close and friendly contact with Swift when he published the poems. His emphasis on Virgil's imitators, rather than on Virgil himself, offers the critic a tremendous advantage. What it does essentially is to free us of the need to speculate on complex relationships between Swift's London and Virgil's golden world—relationships that our preconceptions, and not the poems themselves, tend to press upon us. Now we can look more fully at what in fact is going on within each poem, besides the parody of "fantastical descriptions."

"A Description of the Morning" has as its governing principle the interplay of order and disorder. Whether lowly or exalted, most of the figures who appear in the poem have duties that should contribute to the ordering of their world. Betty, who flies from her master's bed like Aurora from the bed of Tithonus, is presumably a servant-girl with responsibilities for keeping the household in order. The apprentice is supposed to be cleaning the dirt from around his master's door. Moll is caught with her mop in midair, just prepared to scrub. The "Youth with Broomy Stumps" (9) could be sweeping, rather than scavenging in the rubbish. Turnkeys and bailiffs have the job of seeing that society—like houses, stairs, streets, and chimneys—is kept clean. His Lordship, at the apex of his world, has the most pressing duties of all.

Most of these figures responsible for preserving order are actively engaged in disrupting it. The apprentice scatters the dirt as fast as he "pares" it away. The turnkey, a modern shepherd with a convict flock, promotes crimes for his own profit. His Lordship, who should be supervising the work of social sanitation, is hiding from his creditors. Even the bailiffs, within the limits of the poem, do no more than stand in silence. But at the same time, with the breaking of dawn, as real order appears in its death-throes, a false impression of order is coming alive. Betty is returning to her own bed, and the convicts are returning to prison. Swift's irony reaches the highest level of complexity in the case of the servant-girl. Participating in an illicit relationship that reflects the general disorder, Betty preserves the illusion of order by disordering her bed.

Swift seems to suggest that radical disorder is the state of this world, and the best that can ever be attained is a frail and unstable impression of order. He emphasizes the sense of disorderly flux by catching all his characters at a transitional moment, when the reality is just coming into contact with the respectable illusion. The moment comes at dawn—the transition between night and day. Betty is between beds. The apprentice has hardly started on his real work. Moll is merely "Prepar'd" (8) to scrub; and interestingly enough, she is prepared only for the entry and the stairs— the most visible and public parts, the avenues, into disorderly houses. The youth is just beginning to trace the kennel-edge. Duns are beginning to gather at his Lordship's door. Moll has screamed through only half a street. The turnkeys, the bailiffs, and the schoolboys have as yet no idea what the night has brought or the day will bring.

Why this interest in the beginnings of things, in the dynamics of a situation rather than in static pictures? Why focus on a particular moment? Steele has indicated that Swift is concerned with "the incidents just as they really appear." Perhaps things as they are appear in their truest light when shown in contrast to what they are not. And they are not orderly, complete, static, or even necessarily moral.

Yet listening as hard as he can to the lines themselves—without imagining Virgil very close to the scene—the reader hears no notes of rancor, censure, or judgment. The primary clue to the proper reception of this poem is simply the absence of any disparaging comment from Swift. The humor is closer to joie de vivre than to satire: the slipshod apprentice is merely funny, not subject to Alecto's whip. The poem contains no focused objects of blame—a prerequisite to satire. Whom is the reader to accuse, Betty, or her master? The turnkey, or the prisoners? The whole city? What for? In speaking nostalgically of the lagging schoolboys, in a line reminiscent of Shakespeare's "Ages of Man," Swift mixes the clearly innocent with the dubious. The listing procedure, in which this is the last element, implies equality: screaming Moll is no more disgusting than a reluctant schoolboy. As for the screaming itself, it might well have been music to Swift's ears. London street cries interested him so much that he wrote half a dozen delightful imitations of them. Take this example from "Oysters":

> Charming Oysters I cry,
> My Masters come buy,
> So plump and so fresh,
> So sweet is their Flesh,
> No *Colchester* Oyster,
> Is sweeter and moyster,
> Your Stomach they settle,
> And rouse up your Mettle,
> They'll make you a Dad
> Of a Lass or a Lad;   (1–10)

The cries of Brickdust Moll, the "Cadence" of the Smallcoal-Man (11), and the "Shriller Notes" of the Chimney-Sweep (12) make up the kind of urban symphony that Swift could find charming. Details like these, realized so vividly, work with the other evidence to prove this poem is not about hating London: we must assume that a man who listened so carefully and saw so clearly rather enjoyed things as they really were.

Despite Swift's opinion (*Journal,* Vol. 1, p. 109) and the opinions of some critics that "A Description of a City Shower" is a better poem than "A Description of the Morning," it seems to me less well integrated and coherent. "City Shower" does not stand very well on its own, as a poem independent of other poems: Swift was likely so conscious of the virtuoso effect of the particularized parody that he emphasized that aspect. The famous triplets in imitation of Dryden (with the note Swift appended to the Faulkner edition in 1735) are clearly parodic:

> Sweepings from Butchers Stalls, Dung, Guts, and Blood,
> Drown'd Puppies, stinking Sprats, all drench'd in Mud,
> Dead Cats and Turnip-Tops come tumbling down the Flood. (61-63)

The Virgilian simile, comparing the beau boxed in a chair with the Greeks inside the Trojan Horse, probably alludes as much to Dryden's translation of Virgil as to Virgil himself. But the whole organization of the poem, dependent upon the storm scene in the first Georgic, commands a degree of attention to Virgil. And yet, the reader will find upon examination that the classical allusions do not provide a negative commentary on city life.

Offsetting the recollection of Virgil's rural paradise is recognition of Swift's personal involvement with the sights and sounds of the poem. The poet's basic allegiance to the city of London appears even more fully than in "A Description of the Morning," because he clearly rejects the role of distant observer. In describing the stink of London life, which has to be one of its more disgusting aspects, Swift uses "you" to define his stance toward the city:

> Returning Home at Night, you'll find the Sink
> Strike your offended Sense with double Stink.
> If you be wise, then go not far to Dine,
> You'll spend in Coach-hire more than save in Wine. (5-8)

"You" implies not a division between author and reader but a coming together as "we"—this is the sort of smell that all of us Londoners must learn to live with—and "you" in this sense takes the sting out of the satire, as Swift, an Irishman, identifies himself as an urban Englishman. To point the notion he includes a portrait of himself as a fellow citizen:

> Ah! where must needy Poet seek for Aid,
> When Dust and Rain at once his Coat invade;
> His only Coat, where Dust confus'd with Rain,
> Roughen the Nap, and leave a mingled Stain. (27-30)

How exasperating is the life we Londoners put up with! Such a grousing, yet tender, tone is the only one appropriate to these lines, which are in tone rather like "Horace, Lib. 2. Sat. 6" ("I often wish'd, that I had clear"). In both poems the subtle note of self-satisfaction means more than the overt message.

The *Journal to Stella* shows that both Swift and Stella were conscious of his gradual alienation from Irish affairs and assimilation into English culture. In 1710, just before writing "City Shower," he states conscientiously, but without much truth, that he has avoided referring to "you" Irish and "we" English: "I think I am civiller than I used to be; and have not used the expression of (*you in* Ireland) and (*we in* England), as I did when I was here before, to your great indignation" (*Journal,* Vol. 1, p. 47). In the same year his seeming disaffection from Ireland provokes Stella to retaliate: "Insolent sluts! because I say Dublin, Ireland, therefore you must say London, England: that's Stella's malice" (p. 67). Swift actually did feel pangs of homesickness and was not without his moments of pastoral nostalgia. Whoever reads his tribute to Laracor, the site of his vicarage, will not doubt his appreciation for country beauty: "Oh, that we were at Laracor this fine day! the willows begin to peep, and the quicks to bud. My dream's out: I was a-dreamed last night that I eat ripe cherries.— And now they begin to catch the pikes, and will shortly the trouts (pox on these ministers), and I would fain know whether the floods were ever so high as to get over the holly bank or the river walk; if so, then all my pikes are gone; but I hope not. . . . And then my canal, and trouts, and whether the bottom be fine and clear?" (p. 220). But Stella was still basically correct in her fears.

At the time Swift wrote "City Shower," he had just succeeded in finding a niche among some of the most famous and urbane Englishmen of his age, and he was anxious to show that he was one of them. His almost fanatic concern for the poem's reception in Ireland suggests that, simultaneously, he was directing it to his countrymen, as a local boy making good. The geographic detail of the description of London, with its almost maplike quality, would have impressed on the Irish the intimacy of his knowledge. Indeed, no lines illustrate his familiarity with London better than those in the last stanza, including the triplet that parodies Dryden. The torrents drive from Smithfield or St. Pulchre's, join at Snow-Hill

Ridge, fall from the Conduit to Holborn-Bridge, and sweep with them the offal of city life, immortalized in repellent detail. Swift had more than Dryden on his mind.

Besides the sense that Swift feels at home in London, the reader has the more general impression that, in this poem at least, all Londoners are at one. This impression, again, offsets whatever tendency may exist to view Virgil as a negative commentator on the scene. If "A Description of the Morning" embodies joie de vivre, another phrase, esprit de corps, serves as well to convey the predominant mood of "City Shower." Bedraggled females fly "in Crouds" (33) to shops, where they unite in the pretense of bargaining while intending only to find shelter. All the individual acts of fleeing the storm, Swift seems to say, end in the amicable union of strange bedfellows:

> Here various Kinds by various Fortunes led,
> Commence Acquaintance underneath a Shed.
> Triumphant Tories, and desponding Whigs,
> Forget their Fewds, and join to save their Wigs. (39–42)

The fury of the storm makes human fury trivial and breaks down human barriers. In this sense, London temporarily assumes one of the qualities of Paradise: it is blessed, for the moment, not damned.[7]

Nevertheless, with nature at war with man, "City Shower" conveys almost as strong an impression of disorder as "A Description of the Morning." Formal elements in both poems function partly to control impending disintegration. The alliteration in the first line of the earlier "Description" works to counter disorder as much as it works parodically: "NOW hardly here and there an Hackney-Coach . . ." Swift did not simply ignore conventions like alliteration, he actively rejected them, and in doing so put them to good use. His reliance on heroic couplets in both poems rather than octosyllabic verse lends an aura of formality, especially since the poems tend to move line by line and couplet by couplet. The lines are end-stopped more often than usual in Swift, and the couplets closed. Swift seems at pains to provide static frames for his dynamic pictures. The formal stasis gives a counterbalance to the substantive chaos. In other ways, however, it sharpens the sense of disorder. The vignettes in "A Description of the Morning" are only very tenuously related to one another. The effect of "listing" is to stress the individuality of each picture. Every object and character seems distinct, in all its internal disorder and disjunction from the rest of its world. Though a spirit of union appears in "City Shower," the "listing" has its effect here too: the common purpose of the characters is obscured by their very different styles of flight from the storm. Despite some elements of union in "City Shower," and despite the formality of the verse, which partially controls the chaos it contains, in both poems radical disorder ultimately prevails.

How could Swift survey these scenes without animosity? Biographers tell us he was an orderly man, who kept his accounts meticulously. To explain his pleasure in pictures of chaos, let us adapt a phrase from Samuel Johnson's "Preface to Shakespeare" and say that his mind could only repose on the stability of the real. Swift was a man of strong prejudices, who preferred to take sides when he could, but he was also an honest man, who looked at all situations from different perspectives. With a low tolerance for ambiguity, he nevertheless wrote an extraordinary number of ambiguous pieces. In "On Poetry: A Rapsody," the poet is at once heroic and ridiculous. In "Strephon and Chloe" (1731), the object of blame shifts to the point of inconsistency. In the "Digression on Madness" in *A Tale of a Tub,* reason and delusion alternately receive the commendation. In *An Argument against Abolishing Christianity,* proposing to establish *real* Christianity is as absurd as it is desirable. The "Mad Projector" in *A Modest Proposal* finally makes a rather convincing case for the idea that cannibalism is a humane solution to Irish poverty. The political projectors in the Academy that Gulliver visits entertain ludicrous notions about providing princes with wise counselors. And in all Swift's pieces on the writing of satire, he describes it as a very dubious profession. The reader has, in each case, the peculiar sense that Swift will not compromise by choosing A and B, nor will he choose between them. His preference vacillates continually between *A* and B on the one hand, and A and *B* on the other.

W. B. Carnochan's complex and solid view of Swift's vertiginous irony in *A Tale of a Tub* helps to clarify the problem of how Swift could remain merry while writing his chaotic "Descriptions."

Swift's use of minute and vivid detail, his preoccupation with strikingly offensive details, his jokes about excrement, and his omnipresent lists—all mitigate for him the horrific effects of his nihilistic vision.[8] The objects and characters in the two "Descriptions" are tangible, concrete, unambiguous. They are, as Steele would say, things as they really are. Swift's mind, so often tormented by elusive truths, reposes for a moment upon the stability of the real.

The same bent of mind that found rest in the gutters of the two "Descriptions" may have influenced the development of Swift's style in both prose and poetry. The man who could define style as "Proper Words in proper Places"[9] was thinking of words as concrete, manipulatable units. In praising the clear, smooth, masculine style of the Brobdingnagians, Gulliver reflects Swift's own opinion. He says specifically that the Brobdingnagians' style is not florid because they avoid multiplying unnecessary words and using "various" expressions.[10] The idea of language pruned and streamlined implies that Swift viewed words as concrete, and proper style as a fixed ideal, distinct from personality and substance. The Houyhnhnms, similarly, have a Germanic concept of language formation: they create the word for an evil attribute, for example, by combining the word *Yahoo* with another nonabstraction.[11] They define a lie as having said the *"thing which was not."*[12] Significant in this definition, besides the notion that they know "what was," is the word *thing* with the implication, once again, of tangibility. The words Gulliver uses in praising their poetry are completely consistent with Swift's definition of style: Gulliver stresses their "Justness," their "Minuteness," and their "Exactness."[13] In Book III of *Gulliver's Travels,* Swift makes fun of the prose style endorsed by Bishop Sprat of the Royal Society, whereby the name of a thing should in itself reveal its nature. He shows the projectors in the school of languages communicating by means of the cumbersome objects they carry around.[14] Nevertheless, his own concept seems to have developed along the same lines, for his definition of style and his praise for the styles of others emphasize the "thingness" of words.

The concreteness of the two "Descriptions" allowed Swift a respite from the tension of the massive ambiguities he confronted. His style is so artless and simple at first glance, so apparently free of complexities, so solidly grounded in the most tangible kind of language, that it must have offered him the same sort of relief. It is hardly necessary to point out that he was not a simple man with a simple vision. But one will perceive complexity only as one moves further from the words themselves, only after the language has passed by, after the reading is finished and the book set aside. Then comes the struggle with the profundity of Swift's vision. For writers whose style is not clear or smooth or masculine, but florid, Swift has the utmost contempt. In poetry, especially, he presents his alternative.

5. The Stella Poems

We know that Swift felt revulsion against conventional poetic forms. Why then did he write poetry at all? Each poem requires a different answer, but two general reasons suggest themselves—that he was trying to correct tradition by reworking it, and that he was underlining his own sincerity and the worth of his subject by recasting genres suspect in most readers' minds. The poems to Stella, for example, sound more sincere because they are unlike conventional poetic compliments to ladies.

His interest in developing an original form of compliment was stirred by his realization that the old love language had lost its force and freshness. "To Stella, Who Collected and Transcribed his Poems" (1720) shows that he dislikes references to "*Cupid's* Darts" (11) and "killing Eyes" (12) and "bleeding Hearts" (12) because they are trite. He implies that the terms are also empty. The poet may have money, not his mistress, on his mind:

> A Poet, starving in a Garret,
> Conning old Topicks like a Parrot,
> Invokes his Mistress and his Muse,
> And stays at home for want of Shoes:
> ("To Stella, Who Collected and Transcribed his Poems," 25–28)

Or the terms may be empty because they are associated with the Restoration poetry of seduction, where they are so many counters in the love game. The purpose of such terms in Dorset and Sedley and Rochester is not so much praise as persuasion, and Swift resents the kind of cynicism that invokes "Goddesses" to induce deviltry. In "To Stella, Who Collected and Transcribed his Poems," he lists the present sordid lodgings of Chloe, Silvia, Phillis, and Iris. His list records the outcome of these seduction poems.

Swift hates the old love language, then, because it is trite, insincere, and effectively immoral. He hates it too because it describes women hardly worthy of writing about in poetic style. If his list implies that Chloe was seduced, it means as well that she was susceptible to seduction. The goddesses of Restoration love poetry were scarcely flawless even before they met their Restoration lovers. They were women

> Whose Scoundrel Fathers would not know 'em,
> If they should meet 'em in a Poem.   (51–52)

Dorset and Sedley and Rochester might not have cared whether their mistresses deserved praise. They had other interests. But Swift, with his vigorous personal regard for the truth and his hardy Augustan regard for the subject, cares very much that these heroines are degenerate. For him, the Restoration poets praised the wrong women, for the wrong reasons, in the wrong way, and for the wrong things. They praised them, naturally enough, for their beauty and their "kindness," not for their virtue:

> All that in woman is ador'd,
> In thy dear self I find;
> For the whole sex can but afford
> The handsome and the kind.   (Sedley, "Song," 1672)[1]

Swift would have answered Sedley by citing the example of "Maevius" in "To Stella, Who Collected and Transcribed his Poems": his nymph had lost her nose before the poem was complete. Swift's disgust with the physical praise of women in poetry provides a motive for two of his most virulent poems, "A

Beautiful Young Nymph Going to Bed" (1731) and "The Progress of Beauty" (1719).

He evokes the tradition of compliment to ladies and either dismisses it with ridicule or transforms it into something he can approve of. The name he chooses for Hester Johnson sets up the ridicule, for "Stella" reminds the reader of Sidney and all those poetical goddesses with names ending in *a*, who frequented England in the golden time. The references to nymphs and swains also recall the complimentary tradition and clash bathetically with the fact that Stella is fat and thirty-four (or even thirty-eight!). Swift proves to the reader that he can write a better compliment than his predecessors, because he takes actuality into account and still manages to indicate that Stella is twice as beautiful and twice as wise as any other woman. At the same time, he proves to Stella that he loves her, for the compliment absorbs so much of the insulting truth that it must be sincere. Besides, Stella would know that in the course of teasing, one veers so close to insult only with people one loves and trusts. The complimentary strategy is the same in the Stella poems as in "Epistle to a Lady." It is Swift's primary rhetorical device for pleasing women he loves.

His ridicule extends to all the trappings of the complimentary tradition, even to the traditional claims about inspiration and originality. The first stanza of "Stella's Birth-Day. A great Bottle of Wine, long buried, being that Day dug up" (1723), presents the poet biting his nails and scratching his head, unable to write well because "Long-thinking" (12) hinders the work of his imagination. The lines call up another picture—Astrophel in Sonnet 1 biting his pen and beating himself for spite because his powers of "Invention" flag under the blows of "Study." The reader expects Swift's muse to intervene with advice that he look in his heart and write, but the idea of inspiration is too high-flown for his taste, and the claim to originality has been too much abused. He substitutes alcohol for the promptings of the muse and implies, as in *A Discourse Concerning the Mechanical Operation of the Spirit*, that the spring of inspiration is more a mechanical coil than a metaphysical fountain. The appearance of the muse is a hallucination common to rhyming drunkards, and the real motive for summoning the muse is not so much love as reputation. Though Swift jokes about his own sincerity, he really means to question the intentions of poets in general:

> Nor do I ask for *Stella*'s sake;
> 'Tis my own Credit lies at Stake.   (31–32)

He corrects the tradition by redefining its favorite terms, as well as by ridiculing it. "To Stella, Who Collected and Transcribed his Poems" begins with a traditional assertion that all the merit and the praise of the poetry should be Stella's. Shakespeare makes the same claim for his friend in Sonnets 78 and 84, and Sidney gives the praise to his Stella in Sonnets 74 and 90. But where Shakespeare and Sidney claim that the immortal beauty and grace of their subjects make their poems immortal, Swift explicitly dissociates Stella and his poems from such qualities. Stella deserves the credit if his poetry endures, because it reflects her virtue—not because it reflects the accidentals of appearance. In the same poem he recalls the Petrarchan commonplace that Cupid takes up residence in the poet's heart ("I ne'er admitted Love a Guest," 14) and says he is "possesst" (13) by friendship and esteem rather than by the demon love. He transforms all the love motifs he uses. Stella, visiting him in his sickness, comes with cordials in her eyes, but Swift is not sick with a courtly malady and Stella's eyes shine with a different kind of love. Her good sense, not her beauty, breaks like the sun from behind a cloud. She tends him like a slave, but the servitude is that of friendship.

Stella is an angel too—alternately the sign and the hostess of the Angel-Inn. But she is not quite so ethereal as her counterparts in the Renaissance and Restoration. The poet endows her with all the humanity of a good-natured barmaid. His hail-fellow attitude in "Stella's Birth-day. Written AD. 1720–21" will remind some readers of Prior's "Jinny the Just" and Dorset's "bonny black Bess." Dorset's "Song," 1673, shows that even a cavalier could tire of the pastoral conventions. His boredom with Phyllis and Chloris and his preference for Bess points to a traditional analogue for Swift's hatred of this tradition: the poet's conventional claim to sincerity runs without break from Petrarch to the cavaliers. Swift's way of praising Stella is not altogether unlike Shakespeare's method in Sonnet 130:

My mistress' eyes are nothing like the sun,
Coral is far more red, than her lips red,

. . .

And yet by heaven I think my love as rare,
As any she belied with false compare.[2]

And Swift's transformation of the old love terms is not dissimilar to Donne's procedure in "The Dampe" and "The Dreame." Donne tries to persuade his lady by redefining "honor." She will be "brave" and "pure" and truly "angelic" if she consents, but not if she refuses him.

Swift chooses to play with the very same idea, "honor," in his poem "To Stella, Visiting me in my Sickness" (1720). He deliberately leads the reader to believe that he is about to treat feminine honor in the traditional sense, for he says that Pallas, seeing Stella's beauty, must fix honor in her mind to prevent the disruption of the state. For the benefit of a stupid vicious age, he explains that he has in mind neither the courtly female virtue nor the courtly male virtue, neither chastity nor the "Quarrels of a Rake" (24). He means, instead, the kind of fair-dealing characteristic of the Augustan good man. The idea includes chastity, but only by implication. In using loaded language in a new way, Swift—like Donne—is trying to disengage himself from the false assumptions of the past, trying to discover new values that will last because they are more honest and more viable than the old. In rejecting poetic cant, he—like Shakespeare and all the other poets of the love tradition—is trying to make his poetry sound more sincere. His methods of proving that he is honest have precedents in the very tradition he wants to escape. The claim to sincerity is itself part of the cant.

How is Swift to prove that he is any more honest than his predecessors? He severs himself from the tradition, in part, by developing a positive and disinterested alternative to the traditional set of values. Where most love poets stand to gain by their praises, he is not suspect. He compliments Stella for asexual virtues. His emphasis falls on qualities usually associated with men. He comically suggests that the gods mistook Stella's sex when they allotted virtues to her. It is a strange suggestion, and one which recurs in "Cadenus and Vanessa." Like Swift's comparisons of Lady Acheson to a skeleton, devoid of any sexual characteristics, the "masculinity" of these women, his pupils and very much his junior, might have shored up the formal relationship between himself and them by helping him to forget their sexual identity. Whatever its psychological function, the idea may be a necessary step away from usual kinds of poetic condescension. This emphasis on masculine qualities and the contrast he draws between Stella's patience and his own "unmanly" (99) complaints neutralize any sexual possibilities. Instead of aiming at seduction, the poet is presenting a pattern for female behavior which is as much a pattern for all human behavior.

Swift is departing from most love poets, but not from John Donne. He exaggerates Donne's implications and puts his assumptions into unambiguous form. In doing so, he does subvert the whole purpose of the Renaissance poet. Donne surely never intended that his real respect for women should get in the way of a seduction. But his respect, like Swift's, was real. Marvell, at first glance even more different from Swift than Donne, shared with these two the uncavalier quality of respecting women. All three talk to women in a serious way, to the credit of their mistresses and the advantage of their poems. In addressing Stella, as in writing octosyllables, the untraditional Swift had a place in tradition.

His attitude toward women has frequently been the focal point for unfriendly critics. More than his coarseness or his violence, his supposed hatred of women has made him infamous among the "softer-hearted," "better adjusted" men who have condemned him. Thackeray was simply putting into words a bit of common mythology when he asserted that Stella and Vanessa died of broken hearts, abused and neglected by Swift.[3] Psychoanalysis has replaced sentimentalism and added a new twist to Swiftian biography. Now investigators concentrate on sexual quirks—his anality, his homosexual impulses, the possibility of impotence. A vague acquaintance with the excremental poems has given many readers the feeling that sickness and perversion tainted all his relationships with women. Amid all this certainty that he was somehow defective, the claim that he had a healthy and enlightened view of women may seem heretical; yet some of the prose—notably his tract on educating women—and many of the poems are proof that his attitude was much less condescending and much more modern than the attitudes of other eighteenth-century writers. Equally heretical may be the claim that he was related to Donne and Marvell; yet in the best of his poems to ladies, Swift shows the same moral and personal seriousness that helps Donne and Marvell convey their appreciation of womanliness. For the dramatic thoughtfulness of "Stella's Birth-Day. March 13, 1726/7" he probably went back to a subtle but important part of metaphysical tradition. The tone suggests "a man and woman quietly reasoning together."[4] It is the same tone that makes effective Donne's "Valediction: forbidding mourning" and Marvell's "Definition of Love."

In the poem to Stella the tender affection may have been all-important to Stella, but another aspect will attract the general reader: its thoroughgoing truthfulness. Instead of reassuring Stella that her death is not close, Swift faces the fact of death and helps her face it too. The comfort he holds out is the thought that her life has been well spent, not that Heaven will reward her for her virtue or recompense her for her pain. He might have taken an easier course, but the poem would have been less frank, less earnest, less strenuous in its honesty. Here, at his best, Swift can rival the greatness of Donne and Marvell. The same strenuous honesty marks the way all of them, at their best moments, talk to women.

Through the literature from 1590 to 1610, one can trace the breakdown of Elizabethan values. Bred in the new modes of irony, disenchantment, and satire, Donne could still manage to retain a degree of beauty in his relationships with women, while refusing to compromise on his view of reality. In talking to a woman, he commonly did not play the love-game according to the rules. When he approached Petrarchanism, in the small group of poems that includes "The Funerall," "The Blossome," and "The Primrose," his realistic temper colored and changed the mode. A second group, including "Goe and catch," "The Indifferent," and "The Flea," parades his cynicism about himself, his mistresses, and love. What I am concerned with here are the poems that have most relation to Swift, like "The good-morrow," "The Sunne Rising," "The Canonization," "Aire and Angells," and "A Valediction: forbidding mourning." Neither particularly idealistic nor particularly cynical, they tend to abuse or transcend

Petrarchan conventions in the course of expressing true passion.

"The Dampe" is almost not a love poem. The conventions that Sidney often used as material for compliment become, in Donne, the source of comedy and criticism. Donne's lady covets her virtue egotistically, and her notions of proper conduct in love have no reference to reality. Her honor is an enchantress and her disdain, a giant. They are figures from romance, part of an archaic world—not part of her as a woman. The constancy and secrecy she requires of him are Petrarchan values, no longer applicable to the real world. His posture might seem cynical, except that he allows himself the luxury of a few romantic touches. Swift tempers his honesty, too, with a comment on Stella's shining eyes (they shine with altruistic devotion), with a comparison to the sun (her good sense breaks from behind the clouds), or a concluding statement of her beauty (even though she's fat). Donne's lover uses his few courtly images in a less adulterated way. He has the lady's picture in his heart, as Sidney's Astrophel has Stella's. He dies for love, and the lady goes on to kill others. Still, the tone is more realistic than rhapsodic, as he gaily inverts the old love conventions and offers, in their stead, his basic frankness.

As one might imagine from Donne's occasional excursions into idealism, he did not always exult over the decay of Elizabethan love. In "Loves Alchymie," he takes a serious and sad look at idealistic love. The voice is that of an experienced essayist and commentator on the world. Angelic women, Shakespeare's marriage of true minds—the whole business is imposture, he says. But he isn't smirking as he speaks. He has really been investigating. He has really tried to validate Petrarchan values and has failed. The pain of the discovery makes the poet more pitiful than sneering. Donne, like Swift, may have wanted to be a thoroughgoing romantic, and sometimes he almost succeeded. Here, however, his commitment to telling a troublesome truth pulls him back to a harsh reality.

"The Dampe" and "Loves Alchymie" provide a background for the reading of real love poems—poems directly to a woman, and not to the world. Intimate and delicate in tone, "The Dreame" nevertheless presents a realistic view of love. Despite the verbal play and the balance, the poem is far from being courtly. When the lady first entered his room, Donne says he thought she was an angel. But he came to realize that she could be truly divine only as herself, a mortal woman:

I must confesse, it could not chuse but bee
Prophane, to thinke thee any thing but thee.[5]

Her coming and staying make her a goddess in the only sense still significant in Donne's world, but her leaving is a fall from divinity. She can be spiritual, free, and brave—all that a Petrarchan mistress is, and more—only by loving and giving. Both her own value and spiritual union with her lover come out of sexual love. And thus Donne preserves important aspects of Petrarchanism. He can sustain a truthful manner even in an intimate love poem like this, but then, he has a new version of love to replace the outmoded beauties of the old. Apart from its sexual aspect, it is much like Swift's. To this new concept—assuming a different kind of respect for the lady and a greater reliance on her intelligence and perhaps on her sense of humor too—honesty is as integral as sex.

In "Loves growth," Donne sets forth a plan for reclaiming Petrarchan love similar to the plan implied by "The Dreame." He muses that his love is less pure than the love of Petrarchan poets. It is not a quintessence, abstract and immutable, but subject to change. He seems at first to be saying that his love is inferior, but in a witty reversal he establishes its superiority along with its capacity for growth. Instead of proving the impurity of love, each new part just makes a new whole. The idea seems to defy Petrarchan tradition. But the phrase "Gentle love deeds" (19) has chivalric associations, and the images of heaven and stars recall the lady as sun among the spheres. He rejects love traditions and then brings them in by the back door. In the end his love is even close to being immutable. The last lines undercut the nature imagery— the cycle of seasons—and assert that for his love, winter has no meaning: "No winter shall abate the springs encrease" (28). Because it grows and sustains each new bit of growth, his love is better than Petrarchan love, even in Petrarchan terms. Like Swift in all the birthday poems, Donne can compliment a lady more effectively when his poetry absorbs and assimilates a potentially threatening truth.

The difference in intention between Swift's poems and these of

Donne should not obscure their similarities. Both poets condemn outmoded ways of complimenting a lady: Swift rejects love conventions as emphatically as Donne here rejects Petrarchanism. They do so for much the same reason: both believe that the love terms do the lady an injustice and misrepresent the real world. With the dismissal of the love tradition comes a whole new style of addressing a lady, a whole new attitude toward what a lady should and should not be told. Swift's raillery takes the truth into account: Stella is fat and middle-aged. Donne can be frank in a basically affectionate poem: his lady is no angel. Both manage to convey love despite a neglect of traditional compliment. Stella's virtue more than makes up for the decrease in her beauty. Donne's lady is herself, and better than an angel in being so. Both poets do not hesitate to discuss serious matters—the nature of love, the meaning of death—with women they respect enough to tell the truth. Because honesty is essential in this kind of love poem, they tell the truth even if the truth is painful to the lady or the poet. Donne's metaphysical imagery does not seem misplaced when viewed as an attempt to be forthright with his mistress. It appeals to her reason and gives a comprehensible analogue for a difficult emotional truth.

Just as Swift may have been drawn to Butler's octosyllabic verse by considering the attitudes and opinions he shared with the Restoration poet, so he may have been more receptive to the tone of Donne's love poetry because he saw some common elements in their lives. Donne, like Swift, was a clergyman. Donne, like Swift, wrote satires. In each case, the clerical role, or at least the Christian bent, colored and conflicted with the impulse toward satire. Not only did Swift doubt the effectiveness of satire, but he also worried about the motives behind it. His "Epistle to a Lady" and his "Day of Judgement" imply that revenge and not reform may prompt the satirist to write. The ideal Christian would presumably approach any subject in a charitable frame of mind. If his Christianity had a tincture of stoicism (and eighteenth-century Christianity often did), anger in response to vice would seem even more improper. The perfect Christian, with his eye on Heaven and his heart convinced of ultimate good, might see vice as trivial; or he might, in the spirit of love, counsel reform and repentance. He would not, like Swift, yield to spasms of rage and lash his enemies as if vengeance were his. Through much of Swift's work runs the suspicion that satire is not morally defensible—a suspicion that finds its counterpart in Donne.

Donne's "Satyre III," probably written when the poet was poised between Roman Catholicism and the Anglican Church, opens with a kind of chiasmus:

> Kinde pitty chokes my spleene; brave scorn forbids
> Those teares to issue which swell my eye-lids;   (1–2)

Pity relates to tears, scorn relates to spleen, and the emotions clearly conflict. If he had felt pity alone, he might have succeeded in the tragic mode of satire, or he might not have tried his hand at satire at all. If he had felt scorn without pity, he might have found laughing satire congenial or, again, he might have dismissed the abusers of religion as too trivial to write about. But the speaker feels both emotions; and the conflict, especially as expressed in the closed pattern of a chiasmus, seems to imply a stasis in the speaker's mind, a recognition that no solution is available. Since he cannot choose a proper mode, whether tragic or laughing, he cannot "be wise" in proceeding to write a satire. If approached in this confusion, the "maladies" might be too deeply entrenched for reform.

> I must not laugh, nor weepe sinnes, and be wise,
> Can railing then cure these worne maladies?   (3–4)

Without answering the question, the poet simply plunges into the subject as if he cannot help himself. Offering no substantive transition, he moves from one rhetorical question about his satire to further unanswered questions about religion. As a whole, the poem is more a question than an answer and provides no solutions to the problems it examines.

Swift would have understood how pity might counter the impulse toward satire, how scorn toward triviality might help to suppress it, and how the two emotions might work against each other to confirm the impossibility of finding a proper voice. As a clergyman-satirist (to some contemporaries, a contradiction in terms), he would have understood the beginning of "Satyre V," Donne's search for a defensible satiric role:

Thou shalt not laugh in this leafe, Muse, nor they
Whom any pitty warmes; He which did lay
Rules to make Courtiers, (hee being understood
May make good Courtiers, but who Courtiers good?)
Frees from the sting of jests all who in extreme
Are wretched or wicked: of these two a theame
Charity and liberty give me.   (1–7)

Though Swift acknowledged the claims of charity, he never tried
to defend his satire as charitable. In refusing such small comfort,
he differed from Donne. But the similarity of their doubts on this
issue, arising in part from the similarity of their professions, might
have stimulated Swift's interest in all the earlier poet's work.[6]

A study of Marvell's satires, unlike a study of Donne's, reveals
no striking parallels to Swift. Swift was occasionally as topical and
particular as Marvell, but he dealt more frequently with broad
moral issues and wrote better poems when he did. Marvell's use of
octosyllabic verse, whether in satiric or in other kinds of poems,
might possibly have attracted Swift's notice, yet Butler clearly
provides a more probable model. In Marvell's best poems, the
complexity of his syntax, the delicacy of his sound effects, and
the subtlety of his word-play encourage the reader to slow down
and savor each line, each couplet. The final rhymes come soft to
the ear because they are preceded by unusual verbal structures and
intricate patterns of sound. These poems define themselves as
artifacts, not as conversations. In comparison with Marvell's
octosyllabic lines, Swift's seem rougher, choppier, more colloquial,
faster in pace. But with all these differences, Swift might have
discovered a similarity: like Swift and like Donne, Marvell seems to
place a high value on realism even in love poetry.

Marvell's insistence on realism in "To his Coy Mistress" accounts
for some of its success, but it has other virtues as well. The clash
between his lady's values and his own creates a teasing tone,
similar to Swift's raillery but much more delicate. The poet
professes that he would be willing to complain along the banks of
the Humber while his mistress wandered along the Ganges, that he
would love her ten years before the flood while she refused him,
that he would spend thousands of years praising parts of her body.
The language is beautiful but so extravagant that it verges on the

comic. Without sacrificing tenderness or persuasiveness, the poet implies that the lady would really appreciate this kind of adulation, and he gently needles her for her desires.

Against the pretty extravagance of the first stanza, Marvell sets the bitter reality of time. Ugly images obtrude: deserts, dust, ashes, and obscene worms replace rubies, hearts, and interminable praises. Marvell is warning his mistress, but he is not threatening her the way Rochester might threaten a lady. He will be affected just as much as she in the horror that will overwhelm them both. Her beauty will be lost, but his song is stilled. Her honor will turn to dust, but his love turns to ashes. At this point in the poem, the hard truth has apparently destroyed all hope for beauty in the world. Actually, it has only exposed the impossibility of the opening ideas.

In the resolution, realism and tenderness come together. As a beautiful woman, the lady receives her due:

> Now therefore, while the youthful hew
> Sits on thy skin like morning dew,[7]

But a couple of violent images perserve the impression of realism. Like birds of prey, the lovers will devour their time—an allusion, perhaps, to the Renaissance notion that intercourse shortened life. A harsh image of defloration comes near the close:

> And tear our Pleasures with rough strife,
> Thorough the Iron gates of Life.   (43–44)

Marvell, like Donne and Swift, has found a way of pleasing a lady without lying to her. His praises may satisfy her vanity, but his ultimate insistence on the facts of death and violence persuade more effectively by proving him sincere.

Attributed to the author of a seduction poem, "sincere" might seem a strange term. But Marvell makes no promises he cannot keep. He does not offer immortality, or even marriage. He offers a moment of pleasure in a world beseiged by time. The threat of age and death is at least as appalling to him as to his lady. His reflections on what will happen to him with the passage of time make his poem atypical in the *carpe diem* tradition, which generally concentrates on provoking fears in the lady. The poem is not wholly strategic: it is in part a meditation. In the simple rejection of high-flown compliment, Marvell may come close to any number of seduction poets, for anti-Petrarchanism had in his time become a strategy itself. The proof that he is unusual rests primarily on his fears for himself.

If the reader can forget for a moment that they differ in purpose, he will see that all three poets talk to their ladies in much the same way they might talk to a close male friend. They speak quietly, frankly, rationally about very significant matters. Their manner of speaking tends to set them apart not only from their contemporaries but from most of the poets of all ages. Whatever Swift's sexual quirks, however peculiar his relations with Stella and Vanessa, he shared with these notably "healthy" men an uncommon respect for women. Even his raillery implies respect: because of its indirection and its insulting surface, it calls for an intelligent, sensitive, and loving reader. A serious poem like "Stella's Birthday" (1726/7), credits a woman almost too much: it insists upon truths that most people are simply unable to bear. The emphasis on esteem never diminishes the tenderness and kindness of the poetry. Like Donne and Marvell, Swift was a loving teller of truths.

Along with these two Renaissance poets, he developed a new attitude toward women that helped set him apart from his insincere predecessors. But he had a stylistic alternative to offer too —a new and simpler kind of poetry. Before Swift, most love poets talked about simplicity. They even managed to maintain it through whole poems. They resorted to the old conventions, however, when the old conventions seemed to suit their purpose. Sidney scorns Cupid's dart in one sonnet and fires it in another. Swift's new poetry, with its accentuated focus on subject matter, presents an example of a style often alluded to and almost never attempted.

He apparently associates this new spare style with prose, rather than with poetry. For him, poetry may carry the taint of the old stratagems. He connects it as firmly with the insincere love tradition as he connects prose with his own feelings:

> Adieu bright Wit, and radiant Eyes;
> You must be grave, and I be wise.

Our Fate in vain we would oppose,
But I'll be still your Friend in Prose:
Esteem and Friendship to express,
Will not require Poetick Dress;

("Stella's Birth-Day," 1725, 27–32)

His contemporaries, drawing perhaps on Hobbes, must have made the same connections between poetry and insincerity, prose and the truth. In "A Better Answer," Prior shows that he agrees with Swift, and both of them might have been thinking of tenets common in criticism. Prior writes:

What I speak, my fair CLOE, and what I write, shews
    The Diff'rence there is betwixt Nature and Art:
I court others in Verse; but I love Thee in Prose:
    And They have my Whimsies; but Thou hast my Heart.[8]

Of course, both men are writing poetry while protesting that they are sincere, but Swift's lines, at least, are prosy. Perhaps he cultivated a deliberately prosaic manner as part of his campaign against dishonest poets. This hypothesis might explain his predilection for making crucial points in monosyllabic lines, for, as Dryden says, monosyllabic lines turn verse into prose.[9]

The prosiness of Swift's verse points to the likeness between his poetic purpose and the purpose behind his prose satires. In writing technically spare poetry, he tries to reach and express the reality of things—the reality that poetic conventions would disguise and poetic formality would understate. This is the impulse that motivates satire, for the satirist strips the trappings off the truth as well, and discovers the reality behind the appearance.

Swift occasionally must have hated the truth and longed for the appearance. His realization that Stella was dying must have made him want to return to the old disguises. In his "Receipt to Restore Stella's Youth" (1725), he uses the love conventions seriously for a moment. He has just compared Stella to a winter-starved cow reviving in the spring, and as the comforting aspects of the simile strike him, he indulges in a lover's daydream. He hopes more for the restoration of her health than for the return of her beauty, but he still uses the old love language. The setting and the case—Quilca and the Cavan squires—are real and familiar to both Swift and

Stella. The passage is full of Swiftian country talk. But the interspersed references to garlands, nymphs, and jetty locks prove that he is in an unusual mood:

> And if your Flesh and Blood be new,
> You'll be no more your former *You*;
> But for a blooming Nymph will pass,
> Just Fifteen, coming Summer's Grass:
> Your jetty Locks with Garlands crown'd,
> While all the Squires from nine Miles round,
> Attended by a Brace of Curs,
> With Jocky Boots, and Silver Spurs;
> No less than Justices o' *Quorum,*
> Their Cow-boys bearing Cloaks before 'um,
> Shall leave deciding broken Pates,
> To kiss your Steps at *Quilca* Gates;   (37–48)

The dream is, after all, only a dream, and the unrealistic parts of the passage are therefore admissible. Swift is not one to indulge a dream forever. The moment passes quickly and leaves the reader, again, with his own spare style.

Though the prospect of Stella's death could drive him in the direction of conventional compliment, he seems to have been much more comfortable with obliquity. His mode of indirect compliment had its advantages. Stella would never think of him as a parrot of insincere and hackneyed phrases. She could always regard herself as one whom he loved and trusted enough to treat with "abusive" familiarity. She could value herself the more because he addressed her with raillery. How well did such raillery wear? Could Stella respond with equal delight to poem after poem? She must have felt, after a time, that Swift was withholding something which other women enjoyed from their literary lovers, that his continual raillery expressed a radical aversion to commitment. His mode of compliment took the form of teasing, which can indicate an unwillingness to *declare* love. Such a declaration need not have been trite, like the love poems he hated, or even stilted, like that of "Cadenus and Vanessa." He could have found an acceptable way of declaring love before, and not after, Stella reached the point of impending death. He did not make the declaration when it would have had its fullest practical value. That he did not suggest an inadequacy in the poet or in the relationship which the woman who loved him would have sensed.

Teasing implies the withholding of something besides commitment. Raillery, however affectionate, is a form of suspended aggression. Stella must always have felt, in reading the poems, that Swift could hurt her if he wanted to. In one sense he was dangling a carrot. In another, he was arresting the downward swing of an ax. These darker aspects do not obscure the primary impression of genuine love. They do reveal the complexity, and perhaps the ambivalence, of his feelings in his most significant relationship with a woman. Swift was entirely capable of desiring to hurt women. The excremental poems show that, and they show, as well, an extreme anti-Petrarchan bias that the Stella poems scarcely begin to approach. These excremental poems—with their mixture of literary anti-Petrarchanism and hostility toward certain kinds of women—cast light on the Stella poems, which contain a subtler version of the same mixture.

6. The Excremental Poems

Swiftian critics may have done the author a disservice in considering the excremental poems as a unit.[1] Those unfriendly to the poet, like Aldous Huxley and Middleton Murry, have fastened on the shocking imagery common to the poems and explained them all in terms of Swift's perversions.[2] Those who would find a literary justification for the imagery, like Herbert Davis and Irvin Ehrenpreis, have assumed that a single theory can account for the literary purpose in all the poems. Davis thinks that the excremental poems are parodic inversions of sentimental cant: "The whole significance of these poems lies in the fact that Swift hated the sentimentality of the ordinary romantic love-stuff."[3] Ehrenpreis chooses the "Beautiful Young Nymph Going to Bed" as the "best example" of the detested poems, and he puts forward his conclusions about the particular poem—that it satirizes fornication and parodies romantic compliment—as if they explained the intentions behind them all.[4]

Fornication is not an issue in "Strephon and Chloe," "Cassinus and Peter," and "The Lady's Dressing Room." And though parody is apparent—at least by implication—in all the poems, it often seems of secondary importance. Swift's intention shifts from poem to poem. At times, it shifts within the same poem. A defense of this group might satisfy the shocked school of criticism better if it set the imagery in specific contexts and showed that in different ways it forwards the poetic purpose.

"The Progress of Beauty" (1719) is a fairly pure example of Swift's parodic play with certain conventions of Renaissance and Restoration poetry. It embodies his negative critique of these conventions, just as the Stella poems embody his positive recommendations for reform. Swift does have an ethical point to make: his heroine is a whore and her syphilitic decay is a reflection and an effect of her moral deficiencies. But the reader is left not so much disturbed at the moral indictment as gleeful at the destruction of a foolish form of art.

Swift names his "beauty" Celia to show her affinities with that mass of goddesses who swarmed over England in some better day—the goddesses enrolled, he says in "To Stella, Who Collected and Transcribed his Poems,"

> In *Curll*'s Collections, new and old,
> Whose Scoundrel Fathers would not know 'em,
> If they should meet 'em in a Poem.   (50–52)

Wherever the reader might expect a romantic compliment, he finds a dramatic insult instead. He expects an inventory of feminine charms, and he finds "Crackt Lips, foul Teeth, and gummy Eyes" ("The Progress of Beauty," 15). He expects the conventional floral tribute, and he finds

>   For instance; when the Lilly slipps
> Into the Precincts of the Rose,
> And takes Possession of the Lips,
> Leaving the Purple to the Nose.   (25–28)

He looks, perhaps, for an allusion to the chaste Diana, but he finds that Celia resembles her in quite another respect:

>   When first Diana leaves her Bed
> Vapors and Steams her Looks disgrace,   (1–2)

This opening allusion sets the tone for the literary mockery, and each subsequent echo of the classical culture reminds the reader

of the heroic values—in their pristine state and in their debasement
at the hands of poetic fops:

> Thus after four important Hours
> Celia's the Wonder of her Sex;
> Say, which among the Heav'nly Pow'rs
> Could cause such wonderfull Effects.   (53–56)

The reader will not find the poem "merry," exactly, but he will
find it playful and unusually free, for Swift, of moral judgment.
The narrator intervenes between Swift and his material to relieve
him of the necessity of judging the heroine at the end. The narrator may, in fact, give point to the literary satire by providing a
caricature of the poetic gallant. He seems to try very hard to discover matter for a compliment, admiring the ease with which Celia
refurbishes her face. He offers her sympathetic advice—

> Ah Lovely Nymph be not too rash,
> Nor let the Beaux approach too near.   (67–68)

He offers his unpleasant observations with periphrastic delicacy—

> The Black, which would not be confin'd
> A more inferior Station seeks   (33–34)

And he refuses to admit that the moon and Celia suffer from a
disease he refuses to name:

> But Gadbury in Art profound
> From her pale Cheeks pretends to show
> That Swain Endymion is not sound,
> Or else, that Mercury's her Foe.
>
> But, let the Cause be what it will,
> In half a Month she looks so thin   (93–98)

If he comes to prefer "new Nymphs" (120) to Celia, the preference
is precisely what the reader might expect from an insincere and
hyperbolic poet.

The poem is not merely about poets and poetry: a sense of

real ugliness comes through. But the moral point is substantially less important than in other poems. Swift has added caricature to parody to produce a relatively light piece of literary criticism that moves through all the forms of conventional compliment, substituting obscene insults for flattery and leveling satiric blows, along the way, at Partridge and at the pastoral elegy:

> No Painting can restore a Nose,
> Nor will her Teeth return again.   (111–12)

Where is the nose of yesteryear?

The reader may see a few parodic elements in "A Beautiful Young Nymph Going to Bed" (1731)—in the name "Corinna," for example, and in the loving particularity with which she is described. Swift eschewed physical praise in his tributes to female friends like Stella and Biddy Floyd. In the poems to Stella, he even makes fun of her appearance, while praising her intelligence and her disposition. He disliked the elaborate physical descriptions that other poets lavished on their ladies. His poem, in fact, might be a reversal of Donne's elegy to his mistress, "Going to Bed."[5]

Though it has parodic moments "A Beautiful Young Nymph" comes much closer than "The Progress of Beauty" to pure invective against vice. The narrator doesn't scruple to call Corinna what she is:

> Never did *Covent Garden* boast
> So bright a batter'd, strolling Toast;   (3–4)

He does not name her disease, but—

> With gentlest Touch, she next explores
> Her Shankers, Issues, running Sores,
> Effects of many a sad Disaster;   (29–31)

The description has Juvenalian bite, not mitigated by ironic distance:

> Now, picking out a Crystal Eye,
> She wipes it clean, and lays it by.

> Her Eye-Brows from a Mouse's Hyde,
> Stuck on with Art on either Side,
> Pulls off with Care, and first displays 'em,
> Then in a Play-Book smoothly lays 'em.
> Now dextrously her Plumpers draws,
> That serve to fill her hollow Jaws.
> Untwists a Wire; and from her Gums
> A Set of Teeth completely comes.
> Pulls out the Rags contriv'd to prop
> Her flabby Dugs and down they drop.   (11–22)

When Corinna wakes to find her equipment ravaged, the narrator seems for a moment to assume her point of view, as the speaker in "The Progress of Beauty" pretends to assume Celia's:

> *CORINNA* wakes. A dreadful Sight!
> Behold the Ruins of the Night!   (57–58)

But the moment passes quickly. He is only mocking her. He watches her "Anguish, Toil, and Pain" (69) with cold righteousness. The pain is deserved and the toil is misdirected. And unlike the narrator in "The Progress of Beauty," he refuses to admire the effect of her art: "Who sees, will spew; who smells, be poison'd" (74). Swift has taken the same subject and turned it to two different purposes, the literary and the ethical. In "The Progress of Beauty," he replaces romantic compliment with delicate obscenity, as he describes a whore's attempt at beauty. In "A Beautiful Young Nymph," he looks at the same sort of woman and gives a blunt account of the obscenity he sees.

John M. Aden has argued that "A Beautiful Young Nymph" is not the brutal poem it seems, that the descriptive passages are alternately pathetic and absurd: "Except that in the final analysis he holds the two points of view in stubborn equilibrium, his poem tends to move in alternating scenes of grotesque and pathetic emphasis."[6] In making a case for an element of pathos in the poem, Aden cites such expressions as "*mangled*" and "*Anguish, Toil,* and *Pain.*"[7] His conclusion—that "something ultimately pathetic"[8] emerges from the poem—is undoubtedly true, but the pathos lies with the compassionate reader and probably not with Swift. Aden's argument ignores the obvious contempt implied by such lines as "Who sees, will spew; who smells, be poison'd." It rests on the very dubious assumption that Swift could not realize so vividly the sordid details of Corinna's life without commiserating with her. And last, the argument neglects the capacity for harshness in the service of morality revealed in a work like "To Stella, Who Collected and Transcribed his Poems":

> The charming *Silvia* beating Flax,
> Her Shoulders mark'd with bloody Tracks;
> Bright *Phillis* mending ragged Smocks,
> And radiant *Iris* in the Pox.   (45-48)

Here Swift makes a joke of wretched whores, and his intention in "A Beautiful Young Nymph" is probably the same. Any milder interpretation is just an evasion of the truth that his satire can be cruel—the crueler because so rich in detail. Aden's remarks on "A Beautiful Young Nymph" are symptomatic of the modern inclination to fend off the emotional effects of Swift's satire. The need to fend them off is unfortunate for criticism, but it proves indirectly the power of Swift's poetry.

"Cassinus and Peter. A Tragical Elegy" (1731) makes a curious addition to the excremental canon. Unlike "The Progress of Beauty," it takes issue with romantic delusion itself, and not merely with the forms of romantic compliment. The "obscenity" the man sees in his Cælia exposes the folly of his notions about women. It does not, as in "A Beautiful Young Nymph," imply an indictment of her. Cassinus and Peter are young enough and foolish enough to believe in the grand illusions the poets have created for them—the illusion, for example, that women should move on a high spiritual plane and any deflection from the spiritual course is criminal. They meet to discuss love and books— sophomoric love, no doubt, and highfalutin' books. They fancy themselves special wits and lovers. They speak in the language they pick up from the poets, until they have something substantial to say. The unpoetic "Hypps" is almost the only significant word in this passage:

> WHY, *Cassy*, thou wilt doze thy Pate:
> What makes thee lie a-bed so late?

> The Finch, the Linnet and the Thrush,
> Their Mattins chant in ev'ry Bush:
> And, I have heard thee oft salute
> *Aurora* with thy early Flute.
> Heaven send thou hast not got the Hypps.   (29–35)

Swift's contempt for poetic staleness is apparent here and in every allusion to the plundered, worn-out beauties of the classical poets:

> Nor whisper to the tattling Reeds,
> The blackest of all Female Deeds.
> Nor blab it on the lonely Rocks,
> Where Echo sits, and list'ning mocks.
> Nor let the Zephyr's treach'rous Gale
> Through *Cambridge* waft the direful Tale.   (105–10)

But he takes as his primary satiric object the mentality of the rigid romantic, who would sacrifice good sense and good people to preserve his illusions.

Such a romantic might, like Cassinus, see others' defects and neglect his own. Cassy is presented as a masculine Corinna. His horrified charge that "Cælia shits" is hardly appropriate:

> But, such a Sight was never seen,
> The Lad lay swallow'd up in Spleen;
> He seem'd as just crept out of Bed;
> One greasy Stocking round his Head,
> The t'other he sat down to darn
> With Threads of diff'rent colour'd Yarn.
> His Breeches torn exposing wide
> A ragged Shirt, and tawny Hyde.
> Scorcht were his Shins, his Legs were bare,
> But, well embrown'd with Dirt and Hair.
>
>   . . .
>
> His Jordan stood in Manner fitting
> Between his Legs, to spew or spit in.   (9–18, 21–22)

A jordan may have several uses, apparently, but Cassy claims he doesn't need it as a chamber-pot. He swears he's never been guilty of Cælia's crime:

I come, I come,—*Medusa,* see,
Her Serpents hiss direct at me.
Begone; unhand me, hellish Fry;
Avaunt—ye cannot say 'twas I. (85-88)

Romanticism makes Cassy worse than a hypocrite. No natural disaster but excretion seems to faze him. "Death before defecation" is his motto for Cælia. Swift's spoofing only partly disguises his criticism:

DEAR *Cassy,* though to ask I dread,
Yet, ask I must. Is *Cælia* dead?
HOW happy I, were that the worst?
But I was fated to be curs'd. (41-44)

With the same neglect of Cælia's preference, Cassy dismisses the idea of her dishonor or disfigurement with philosophical claptrap:

Say, has the small or greater Pox
Sunk down her Nose, or seam'd her Face?
Be easy, 'tis a common Case.
OH *Peter*! Beauty's but a Varnish,
Which Time and Accidents will tarnish:
But, *Cælia* has contriv'd to blast
Those Beauties that might ever last. (48-54)

The sentiments may be true, but how can Cassy think only of beauty when his friend is talking about small pox and syphilis? Cassy shows himself indifferent to Cælia's death, her injury, and her vice. His obsessive concern with one "virtue" makes him oblivious to all the others:

COME, tell us, has she play'd the Whore?
OH *Peter,* wou'd it were no more! (45-46)

The reader might conclude, from "Cassinus and Peter," that Swift damns the romantic delusion along with its forms of expression, but the matter is not so simple. In "Strephon and Chloe" (1731), Swift continues his attack on the romantic forms. His attitude toward the delusion is highly ambiguous. The poem as a whole is a parodic epithalamium, Swift taking the occasion to deflate romantic poetry:

> ADIEU to ravishing Delights,
> High Raptures, and romantick Flights;
> To Goddesses so heav'nly sweet,
> Expiring Shepherds at their Feet;
> To silver Meads, and shady Bow'rs,
> Drest up with *Amaranthine* Flow'rs.   (197–202)

He satirizes the celebration of physical beauty in lines that contain a whiff of Donne:

> Licence my roaving hands, and let them go,
> Before, behind, between, above, below.
>
> (Donne, "Going to Bed")[9]

> And then, so nice, and so genteel;
> Such Cleanliness from Head to Heel:
> No Humours gross, or frowzy Steams,
> No noisome Whiffs, or sweaty Streams,
> Before, behind, above, below,
>
> ("Strephon and Chloe," 9–13)

But Strephon is no poet, and Swift gives no evidence that he, like Cassinus, admires poetic cant. Strephon simply believes the poetic notions. He believes his lady is a goddess for him to worship and serve.

Swift seems at first to laugh at Strephon for this delusion, as he laughed before at Cassinus:

> *Strephon* had long perplex'd his Brains,
> How with so high a Nymph he might
> Demean himself the Wedding-Night:
> For, as he view'd his Person round,
> Meer mortal Flesh was all he found:
>
>   . . .
>
> While she a Goddess dy'd in Grain
> Was unsusceptible of Stain:
> And, *Venus*-like, her fragrant Skin

Exhal'd *Ambrosia* from within:
Can such a Deity endure
A mortal human Touch impure?   (72–76, 85–90)

Strephon cuts a ridiculous figure in his attempts to make himself
worthy of his love, as ridiculous as Aeneas does beribboned and
perfumed for Dido:

His Night-Cap border'd round with Lace
Could give no Softness to his Face.   (93–94)

He discovers that his lady is no more divine than he in a comic
descent that recalls the fatuous horror of Cassinus ("O! Cælia,
Cælia, Cælia sh--- "):

STREPHON who heard the fuming Rill
As from a mossy Cliff distill;
Cry'd out, ye Gods, what Sound is this?
Can *Chloe,* heav'nly *Chloe* ----?   (175–78)

Strephon cannot escape the effects of the comic clash between
fact and simile—"As from a mossy Cliff." Swift has identified him
with the high-flown notions the poem deflates, and every time the
romantic bubble is burst by a pointed reality, Strephon suffers in
the consequence. Even when Swift denies that the reality fits
Celia, the negation is forgotten in appreciating the vividness of the
image:

Her graceful Mein, her Shape, and Face,
Confest her of no mortal Race:
And then, so nice, and so genteel;
Such Cleanliness from Head to Heel:
No Humours gross, or frowzy Steams,
No noisome Whiffs, or sweaty Streams,
            . . .
Her Arm-pits would not stain her Gown:
At Country Dances, not a Nose
Could in the Dog-Days smell her Toes.   (7–12, 22–24)

The unpleasantness of what is denied remains uppermost in the reader's mind, and that unpleasantness makes Strephon look absurd.

Swift's satiric strategy through the first part of the poem turns on this comedy of elevation and descent—the goddess and the noisome whiffs. At times the narrator pretends a sympathy with romantic ideals to intensify the force of the fall. He hesitates, out of delicacy, and then puts his statement in blunt, slangy words:

> NOW, *Ponder well ye Parents dear;*
> Forbid your Daughters guzzling Beer;
>
>   . . .
>
> SAY, fair ones, must I make a Pause?
> Or freely tell the secret Cause.
>   TWELVE Cups of Tea, (with Grief I speak)
> Had now constrain'd the Nymph to leak.   (115–16, 161–64)

But when, through these devices, Strephon's delusions are finally and completely routed, Swift seems to regret the effectiveness of his satiric maneuvers. He looks around at the wreckage of romantic thought and finds "gross and filthy" everything that has survived:

> TO see some radiant Nymph appear
> In all her glitt'ring Birth-day Gear,
> You think some Goddess from the Sky
> Descended, ready cut and dry:
> But, e'er you sell yourself to Laughter,
> Consider well what may come after;
> For fine Ideas vanish fast,
> While all the gross and filthy last.   (227–34)

The romantic in Swift cries out for happiness and recoils from mockery. The idea that he felt an attraction to romanticism may throw new light on "Cassinus and Peter" if he, as I believe, is there trying to exorcize his own romantic horror at excretion. At any rate, he implies that the writer who turns from romanticism to satire makes a bargain with the devil. When he "sells" himself to laughter, he relinquishes the blessing of being well deceived.

In *A Tale of a Tub* the conception of happiness as Swift defines it has the ring of truth, even though cynical and spoken by a madman: "we shall find all its Properties and Adjuncts will herd under this short Definition: *That, it is a perpetual Possession of being well Deceived*" (*A Tale of a Tub*, p. 171). This is not simple irony, to be understood by inversion. It strikes the reader with conviction, and surprise that a satirist has said it. Swift, as I have said, was never convinced of the value of unmasking. He doubts its effectiveness, but more fundamentally, he thinks it might be better to let well enough alone. In his *Meditation upon a Broomstick,* he compares the reformer to a bungling broom: "And yet, with all his Faults, he sets up to be a universal Reformer and Corrector of Abuses; a Remover of Grievances; rakes into every Slut's Corner of Nature, bringing hidden Corruptions to the Light, and raiseth a mighty Dust where there was none before; sharing deeply all the while in the very same Pollutions he pretends to sweep away."[10] If the romantic delusion is wrong-headed, it is at least a support for happiness, and the dust the reformer raises will bury a comfort along with a lie.

Of course, the Swift of other moods despised delusion. He directs his harshest satire at the self-deluded masses of men who expect salvation in "The Day of Judgement." Gulliver becomes uncontrollably angry when he sees a Yahoo who is proud of himself. Throughout Swift's works runs his scorn for men who allow themselves to be "bit," and he makes Strephon ridiculous in spite of his "fine Ideas." The hopelessness of the last couplet about the vanishing of fine ideas and the survival of everything gross and filthy must affect the reading of all the excremental poems. Though the thought occurs explicitly only in "Strephon and Chloe," the same despair underlies each of them, however funny they may seem, however much concerned with literary forms. This couplet provides the one legitimate way of viewing the poems as a unit as well as another means of understanding why the imagery recurs and recurs. For Swift, excrement becomes the symbol for life's disappointments and defeats.

Why he chose excrement as his primary symbol may relate more to his psychology than to satiric strategy. Nonetheless, I suggest that the reductive potential of the metaphor, its capacity for humbling pride and undermining flimsy social distinctions, came to Swift already proved by such illustrious writers as Aristophanes and Rabelais. Psychoanalysis tells us that anality is the most repressed aspect of human sexuality. No grown man, however boastful of his sexual prowess, is proud of his ability to excrete. The human tendency to repress and deny anality makes its exposure particularly shocking and particularly effective in satire, whether or not the metaphor occurred to the poet for those reasons.

Swift's use of the metaphor illumines to some degree what it represented for him. In his discussion of the Aeolists and in the "Digression on Madness" from *A Tale of a Tub,* he uses excremental imagery to subvert mistaken ideas about inspiration and greatness. *A Discourse Concerning the Mechanical Operation of the Spirit* employs the same imagery, more clumsily, to the same purpose. In Book I of the *Travels,* Gulliver scandalizes the Lilliputian empress by urinating on a palace fire. In Book III, Gulliver himself is scandalized by the filth of mad projectors. In his role as representative of humanity in Book IV, he is humiliated by the scatological revelry of the Yahoos, especially when they use their dung as a weapon against him. Besides the excremental poems, these are the most significant instances of Swift's play with scatology. But is he really playing? The denial of human greatness and even dignity—whether typified by the Aeolists, by the king of France, by the Lilliputians, by mad scientists, by the Yahoos, or by Gulliver—is hardly funny in itself. We know that Swift sometimes inclined toward hero worship, that he idolized Temple and Oxford and Bolingbroke, that he read history with the view that men made it, not that it made them. For him to insist on the degradation of humanity by exposing the humblest of human functions could not have been a painless act. It is the act of a man whose expectations have been blasted by the flaws of his heroes, whose idealism has been shaken by continual disappointment, whose positive values have suffered in conflict with a powerful negative reality. In Swift, the pain lasted, with all the gross and filthy, while he grasped, like Strephon, at the ephemeral fine ideas.

With the vanishing of fine ideas, the up-and-down movement of the poem stops. Swift demands that every wife hide "each Blemish" (253) from her husband. The narrator ceases to assume delicate poses. He ceases to assume any poses at all and merges with the author himself. Swift has a justified complaint to make in behalf of husbands in all ages. Women "take Possession of the Crown, / And then throw all their Weapons down" (261–62). In an article that otherwise helps to clear away the critical debris around the excremental poems, Donald Greene interprets this call to concealment as ironic. The lines invoking "FAIR *Decency*" (219) and summoning "Opinion" to support "Beauty" (223–24) sound to him like an adman's pitch for deodorants or cosmetics.[11] Could a master ironist have meant these stanzas seriously? He could have and probably did.

Though Swift usually loved to tear the mask from the face of vice, he was not above advocating an expedient hypocrisy in support of virtue. Though his attacks on vice may strain the intelligence of the most sophisticated reader, his positive opinions often seem banal and simple-minded. He was not a philosopher, but a satirist. *A Project for the Advancement of Religion and the Reformation of Manners,* where Swift proposes material rewards for virtue and argues that the hypocrisy thus encouraged might have its advantages, presents the same problems and temptations as this passage from "Strephon and Chloe." With some reluctance in both cases, I conclude that the *Project* is serious and that the plea for as much attention to cleanliness and daintiness after marriage as before it provides a sincere balancing center in "Strephon and Chloe." The plea does not eliminate the contradictions.

For the ridicule of romanticism still stands, and the reader is confused by the change in direction. Cleanliness is only sometimes Swift's major concern in the poem. At other moments, the real point at issue is excretion itself. If romanticism is ridiculous, then a woman's natural functions should not be reprehensible, and Strephon's resentment is as unjustified as Cassinus'. (Strephon is objecting not merely to Chloe's lack of discretion. He would be just as dismayed if he discovered her humanness under happier circumstances.) But if a woman's natural functions are blemishes that tell, somehow, against her virtue, then a husband's expectations do not deserve deflation. In "Strephon and Chloe" the satire flies in all directions. Women are at fault for exposing their blemishes and destroying their husbands' illusions. Men are at fault for their ridiculous notions. Women are advised to maintain their "Beauty" by sustaining their husbands' wrong opinions—

> For, Beauty, like supreme Dominion,
> Is best supported by Opinion;
> If Decency brings no Supplies,
> Opinion falls, and Beauty dies.   (223–26)

And men are advised not to build on beauty at all:

> Since Beauty scarce endures a Day,
> And Youth so swiftly glides away;
> Why will you make yourself a Bubble
> To build on Sand with Hay and Stubble?   (303–06)

Swift seems to have lost artistic distance here and introduced the inconsistencies of his personal attitudes into the piece. Romantic delusion is and is not reprehensible, and a woman's excreting is and is not innocent. Beauty is and is not the mainstay of a marriage. The loss of artistic distance argues the presence of a factor or factors deeply disturbing to Swift. Perhaps the contentions of his critics deserve a measure of credence: he may be excessively upset by the idea of excrement even though he makes a joke of it, or his attitude may fluctuate ambiguously between horror and attraction. Either explanation might account for the disruption of this satire as a work of art. But another possibility remains. The man whose whole life was devoted to the destruction of "fine Ideas" would find sufficiently disturbing the realization that "all the gross and filthy last." What the poem acknowledges, painfully, about satire may best account for its inconsistencies.

The narrator offers esteem and friendship as alternatives to an ill-founded passion. His choice of alternatives, with the confession that he has never experienced Strephon's kind of love, confirms the impression that Swift has entered the poem almost too completely. Though Swift knew another kind of love, he was never convinced, intellectually at least, by the attractions of romantic passion. He makes his position explicit in "To Stella, Who Collected and Transcribed his Poems":

> Thou *Stella,* wert no longer young,
> When first for thee my Harp I strung:

. . .

With Friendship and Esteem possesst,
I ne'er admitted Love a Guest.   (9-10, 13-14)

The parallels with "Strephon and Chloe" are obvious. Swift's personal inconsistencies and his personal involvement with the themes of "Strephon and Chloe" must explain the dissipation of his satiric energy, directed here against mutually exclusive objects.

The reader might expect the same problems to arise in "The Lady's Dressing Room" (1730), in which Celia is damned for her violation of romantic forms, and Strephon, who finds her out, is damned for resenting it. Swift takes Celia to task with unprecedented violence:

Now listen while he next produces,
The various Combs for various Uses,
Fill'd up with Dirt so closely fixt,
No Brush could force a way betwixt.
A Paste of Composition rare,
Sweat, Dandriff, Powder, Lead and Hair;
A Forehead Cloth with Oyl upon't
To smooth the Wrinkles on her Front;
Here Allum Flower to stop the Steams,
Exhal'd from sour unsavoury Streams,   (19-28)

But the narrator seems to excuse Celia and find Strephon at fault for holding his discoveries against her:

But Vengeance, Goddess never sleeping
Soon punish'd *Strephon* for his Peeping;
          . . .
I pity wretched *Strephon* blind
To all the Charms of Female Kind;
Should I the Queen of Love refuse,
Because she rose from stinking Ooze?
          . . .
When *Celia* in her Glory shows,
If *Strephon* would but stop his Nose;   (119-20, 129-32, 135-36)

The goddess Vengeance punishes Strephon with the same affliction that makes the narrator in "Strephon and Chloe" unable to love:

His foul Imagination links
Each Dame he sees with all her Stinks:
And, if unsav'ry Odours fly,
Conceives a Lady standing by:
All Women his Description fits,
And both Idea's jump like Wits:
By vicious Fancy coupled fast,
And still appearing in Contrast.[12]   (121-28)

The narrator in "The Lady's Dressing Room," however, recommends indifference to the repulsive discoveries. He claims that he can accept the Queen of Love despite her origins and feels only a joyful surprise at a woman's ability to transform herself:

Such Order from Confusion sprung,
Such gaudy Tulips rais'd from Dung.   (143-44)

Swift has found, in "The Lady's Dressing Room," a device that permits him to accomplish his two satiric purposes at the same time. The invective against Celia is not undermined by the satire on Strephon because the narrator intervenes to make the second point in his own person. His recommendations are ironic in part, and the irony is confirmed by the force and abruptness of the pejorative words:

Because she rose from *stinking Ooze*?

. . .

Such gaudy Tulips rais'd from *Dung*.[13]   (132, 144)

But Swift and Strephon, who is a kind of satirist-figure, would surely take his advice if they could.

Swift plays out the satirist's tragedy in the lady's dressing room. Strephon looks behind the scenes, as Swift himself does in the writing of the satires, and neither can escape into indifference from the burden of his knowledge. If this knowledge is obscene, it can be put to use, nonetheless, in legitimate works of art. It can function as part of a parody or a declamation against vice. It can point up the folly of romantic delusion or the ambiguities of the satiric point of view. Only when the writer seems disconcerted by his own material or unaware of its moral weight will the question of legitimacy seriously arise. "Strephon and Chloe" justly arouses suspicion. So does the use of excrement in "A Panegyrick on the D—n, in the Person of a Lady in the North" (1730). Here, in an apostrophe to the goddess Cloacine, the scatology is sly, coy, devoid of horror. Though grotesque, it verges on the beautiful:

> This earthly Globe to thee assign'd,
> Receiv'd the Gifts of all Mankind.
>
> . . .
>
> The Margin of a purling Stream,
> Sent up to thee a grateful Steam.
> (Though sometimes thou wer't pleas'd to wink,
> If *Nayads* swept them from the Brink)
> Or, where appointing Lovers rove,
> The Shelter of a shady Grove:
> Or, offer'd in some flow'ry Vale,
> Were wafted by a gentle Gale.   (235–36, 241–48)

Jokes like these lack the justification of the other poems. Swift is close to Pope's *Dunciad* here, especially to the lines in Book II where Smedley disports himself among the mud-nymphs, wafting vapors, and tinctured streams. He is also closer in this poem to true coprophilia than he is anywhere else.

But a sober defense of the five primary excremental poems may only obscure what is perhaps their real purpose: some readers will find them very funny. The anxiousness induced by reading them, so long as it does not develop into panic or disgust, will stimulate laughter. A certain degree of unease is not incompatible with humor, and promotes laughter instead of blocking it. The excremental images serve the purpose of comedy by provoking laughter in readers less sensitive to them. On the other hand, since too much nervousness cuts off laughter completely, more sensitive readers will find their sense of humor overwhelmed by their feeling of disgust. Possibly because romantic attitudes toward women still persist in the modern age, more men than women feel that the poems are too shocking to be humorous. Women live with the knowledge of their natural functions and are better able to accommodate themselves to the excremental imagery—a fact that outweighs another which would otherwise produce the opposite result: women are in general less accustomed than men to the

public acknowledgement of these terms.[14] For the reader who can
live with the excremental imagery, however, another obstacle
remains. Ultimately, laughter may be blocked by the real despair
of admitting that "all the gross and filthy last." No one could feel
this despair more than Swift himself, but to some degree all
readers will react to it. If the material were presented by another
writer, Aristophanes for example, the horror and despair might be
tempered by a larger humanity—one that embraced sympathetically both the ugliness and the humanness of man's gross condition.
Presented by Swift, the images and ideas leave readers who cannot
laugh with a sense of hopelessness.

The reader who thinks that excrement, even as a symbol, should
not provoke so strong a reaction might well try to imagine himself
transported back to that time. Seeing what Swift was up against
might change the mind of the hardiest modern. The eighteenth
century considered Swift's sense of cleanliness odd, if not outright
pathological. In habit, in personal delicacy and views of hygiene,
the twentieth century is far closer to him than his contemporaries
were. He was quirkily sensitive to the same things that masses of
men are now trained to consider delicate. If he was peculiar, time
has given him good company.

Modern sensibility.

7. The Poems of Daily Social Life

The excremental poems and the poems to Stella represent the extremes of Swift's style. His poems to and for his friends show him in a more typical mood. A few of the poems approach straightforward praise. The verses "To Lord Harley, since Earl of Oxford, on his Marriage" (1713) are so straightforward and conventional that they are uninteresting, but most of the poems rely upon raillery to convey affection. In his poem "To Mr. Delany" (1718) Swift defines raillery, rather strictly, as a compliment in the guise of an insult. He says that raillery combines humor and wit:

> From both, we learn to Railly well;
> Wherein French Writers most excell:
> Voiture in various Lights displays
> That Irony which turns to Praise,
> His Genius first found out the Rule
> For an obliging Ridicule:
> He flatters with peculiar Air
> The Brave, the Witty, and the Fair;
> And Fools would fancy he intends
> A Satyr where he most commends.   (31–40)

Simple examples of raillery, constructed according to this rule, abound in the poetry and prose. "An Epistle to a Lady" (above, Chapter 1) substitutes raillery for direct praise and so avoids the appearance of flattery:

> THO' you lead a blameless Life,
> Are an humble, prudent Wife;
> Answer all domestick Ends,
> What is this to us your Friends? (99–102)

Among the examples in prose, some of the most moving occur in the correspondence. Swift's compliment to Arbuthnot in July 1714 works in the same way as his compliment to Lady Acheson. He assumes a crotchety pose and seems to begrudge his praise, thereby making the praise more believable. The truth is, by implication, forced out of him: "All your Honor, Generosity, good Nature, good Sense, Witt, and every other Praiseworthy Quality, will never make me think one Jott the better of You. That time is now some years past, and you will never mend in my Opinion. But really Brother you have a sort of Shuffle in your Gate: and now I have s^d the worst that your most mortall Enemy could say of you with Truth" (*Corr.,* Vol. 2, p. 82). By pretending to speak like an enemy, Swift disclaims any prejudice in favor of Arbuthnot and gives his praise the aspect of an objective account.

Swift must have liked this "obliging Ridicule" of Arbuthnot, for he repeated it eleven years later in a letter to Pope. The resulting raillery is possibly the tenderest compliment he ever made, outside of his tributes to Stella: "O, if the World had but a dozen Arbuthnetts in it I would burn my Travells but however he is not without Fault. There is a passage in Bede highly commending the Piety and learning of the Irish in that Age, where after abundance of praises he overthrows them all by lamenting that, Alas, they kept Easter at a wrong time of the Year. So our Doctor has every Quality and virtue that can make a man amiable or usefull, but alas he hath a sort of Slouch in his Walk. I pray god protect him" (Vol. 3, p. 104). The passage is, above all, a compliment, but it is not nearly so simple as the previous two examples. It works according to the same rule, but because of its context it radiates a further significance and proves how complex Swift's raillery can be.

Swift has begun the letter with an ironic reference to the noble scene of Dublin and to his glorious duties in regulating the weight of bread and butter. He follows with what seems to be a misanthropic manifesto: he says that he hates mankind but loves "John, Peter, Thomas and so forth" (p. 103). The credo, however, is riddled with irony. In the first place, the phrase "John, Peter, Thomas and so forth" admits of endless additions and suggests that Swift was making fun of himself, that he saw the logical fallacy involved in hating mankind and loving a succession of individuals.[1] Second, he cautions Pope not to reveal his system— "but do not tell" (p. 103)—in an aside that implies a comic conspiracy and undercuts the seriousness of the passage. And last, the injunction to Pope that he must rally "all honest men" in their support conflicts ironically with all that Swift has said about collections of men. Swift has realized—perhaps even in the process of writing—that he cannot reconcile his theoretical hatred with his inevitable love. The realization takes the form of satire on himself.

The raillery of the Arbuthnot passage saves Swift from the conflict between his theory and his practice. His lament for the doctor's ill health would otherwise subvert his system, for he cannot logically hate all mankind and love Arbuthnot. The raillery preserves the letter of Swift's law because, after all, Arbuthnot has a defect. At the same time, it reinforces the praise (and extends Swift's satire on himself) because the defect is so trivial that only the overscrupulous satirist would ever notice it. Here, the raillery is not merely a joke. It has a serious side. Swift really does not want to acknowledge the existence of a perfect man. He really does not want to burn his *Travels.* For the satirist Swift, Arbuthnot must have his negligible fault just as, for the satirist Gulliver, Pedro de Mendez must have his. Without disavowing his love for Arbuthnot, without ignoring the inconsistency of his theory and his practice, Swift has chosen to affirm the imperfection of mankind.

Arbuthnot could hardly have taken offense at Swift's joking reference to his slouch: that detail is absorbed in the overwhelming praise. But Swift and his friends understood raillery in a looser sense—not only as a compliment in the guise of an insult, but as teasing or banter in general. In theory, teasing might have the same effect as raillery strictly defined, for teasing conveys an assurance of intimacy and compliments by indirection. In practice, however, the teasing sometimes went awry and insult prevailed over compliment. Swift wrote his verses "To Mr. Delany" in order to admonish his friend Sheridan for wounding his feelings and transgressing the rules of raillery.

What rankled with Swift was a poem Sheridan wrote at the beginning of their acquaintance. In *The History of the Second Solomon,* Swift describes the poem: "In three months time, Solomon, without the least provocation, writ a long poem, describing that person's muse to be dead, and making a funeral solemnity with asses, owls, &c., and gave the copy among all his acquaintance."[2] Sheridan was touching on a sensitive issue. Even early in his career, Swift was anxious about the flagging of his poetic genius. Having struck a vein, however, Sheridan mined it for all it was worth, and Swift was harassed more than once with the charge of poetic impotence. In 1718, the same year that Swift wrote "To Mr. Delany," Sheridan wrote in creaky verse:

> OFT have I been by poets told,
> That, poor Jonathan, thou grows old.
> Alas, thy number[s] falling all!
> Poor Jonathan, how do they fall!
> Thy rhymes, which whilom made thy pride swell,
> Now jingle like a rusty bridle:
> Thy verse, which ran both smooth and sweet,
> Now limp upon their gouty feet;[3]   (1–8)

Swift could take a joke as well as any man, but Sheridan's lines gave him no amusement. He feared to criticize Sheridan to his face because, as he explained to Delany, "I may be thought a Man who will not take a Jest" (*Corr.,* Vol. 2, p. 301). Here the friendship might have ended, with Swift unable to voice his resentment, but the very raillery that provoked the quarrel provided the solution. For Swift and Sheridan raillery was not only an expression of friendship, it was an agent of friendship. They worked out their differences in a series of poetic trifles. On October 27, 1718, seventeen days after writing "To Mr. Delany," Swift explained to Sheridan the rationale behind his own name-calling. In the poem "Sheridan, a Goose" (1718), Swift says that the hard names he calls his friend are only evidence of his affection:

Suppose I call'd you goose, it is hard
One word shou'd stick thus in your gizzard.
You're my goose, and no other man's;
And you know all my geese are swans: (9–12)

He implies that his teasing establishes a kind of claim to Sheridan:
"You're my friend, and I'll call you what I please." Sheridan is not
to look for literal meaning in the raillery or gauge Swift's standards
by those of other men, but to take into account his friend's
aversion for fine words and discover the praise buried in the insult.

Sheridan's raillery tended to be cruder than Swift's and his
affection less overt. He replied in good spirits but without much
charm:

Tho' you call me a goose, you pitiful slave,
I'll feed on the grass that grows on your grave. (31–32)

Swift retaliated with a circuitous bit of flattery called "Mary the
Cook-Maid's Letter to Dr. Sheridan" (1718). In part the poem
depends for its humorous effect on conversational rhythms and
absurdly elongated lines. The poet used these devices again in his
verses "From Dr. Swift to Dr. Sheridan" (1719):

IT is impossible to know by your Letter whether the Wine
is to be bottled To-morrow, or no.
   If it be, or be not, why did not you in plain *English*
tell us so?— (1–2)

and the repetition suggests that he was playing a few favorite tricks
on Sheridan. An even closer analogue, however, is "Mrs. Harris's
Petition," for it adds to the unpoetic play a splendid comic
characterization. Swift was definitely retracing old ground, but
"Mary the Cook-Maid's Letter" puts the old tricks to new uses
and manages to flatter Sheridan while seeming to abuse him.

Swift portrays Mary as a pious old woman scandalized by
Sheridan's insults to her master:

Yes; you call'd my Master a Knave: Fie Mr. *Sheridan*,
   'tis a Shame
For a Parson, who shou'd know better Things, to come
   out with such a Name. (5–6)

By making Mary his spokesman, Swift can chastize Sheridan indirectly for his real abuses of raillery. At the same time, he eludes
the charge that he cannot take a joke. Besides wanting Sheridan to
understand the proper limits of raillery, he wants to affirm the
friendship. Saunders, Swift's male servant in the poem, puts both
these sentiments into words. The second line is only semiserious,
but it makes its point:

> My Master is so fond of that Minister that keeps the
>   School;
> I thought my Master a wise Man, but that Man makes
>   him a Fool.   (29–30)

Of course Mary does not understand the proper function of
raillery any more than Sheridan does. She seems to deny that her
master would ever call Sheridan a goose on the grounds that he has
never called her worse than sweetheart; "drunk or sober" (14).
Her simplicity, set off against the sophistication of the two wits,
creates much of the comedy, but Swift in this instance would
probably give a partial endorsement to her belief that "Gentle
folks should be civil" (24). Even Mary, "a poor Servant" (24),
abides by this rule. The funniest line in the poem comes when,
after all her incivilities to Sheridan, she finally takes her leave:
"And so I remain in a civil way, your Servant to command" (38).
The poem maneuvers between seriousness and humor, now assur-
ing Sheridan of Swift's affection, now abusing him, now correcting
his conception of raillery. A fine piece of characterization, this
poem is also the final document in Swift's controversy with
Sheridan and the cleverest means he found of teaching, by
example, what good raillery could be.

A serious discussion of Swift's difficulties with Sheridan probably obscures the amount of sheer fun involved in writing these
trifles. Though Sheridan could wound Swift, he could also give
him joy. A poem sent through the mail or shoved under a door
gives pleasure today among lesser wits than Swift and Sheridan.
These two overwhelmed one another with their jokes and their
proofs of casual poetic skill. Sheridan must have laughed at the
footnote to one of Swift's poems: "I BEG your Pardon for using
my left Hand, but I was in great Haste, and the other Hand was

employed at the same Time in writing some Letters of Business."[4] Sheridan replied by going one better: he wrote his two poetic answers simultaneously with his left and his right hands.[5] Swift prodded his friend on by saying at the end of one of his poems, "Written, sign'd, and seal'd, five minutes and eleven seconds after the receipt of yours."[6] The contest continued, now with riddles, now with rhymes. Swift regarded rhyme, in particular, as his forte, and he once challenged Sheridan and Dr. Helsham with thirty-three rhymes playing on the same sound.

Better poetically, though still trifles, are Sheridan's ballad on the spa at "Ballyspellin" (1728) and Swift's abusive "Answer to the Ballyspellin Ballad" (1728). In a letter to John Worrall in 1728, Swift explained the origin of his poem, and the reader can see between the lines the zest he felt for this kind of game: "We have a design upon Sheridan. He sent us in print a Ballad upon Ballyspelling, which he has employd all the Rimes he could find to that word; but we have found fifteen more, and employd them in abuseing his Ballad, and Ballyspelling to" (*Corr.,* Vol. 3, p. 302). Sheridan's ballad is principally a tribute to the ladies of Bally-spellin, and it sometimes employs the shopworn gallantry that disgusted Swift in the old poets. Death, says Sheridan, throws no darts,

> Except you feel Darts tipt with Steel,
>   Which here are ev'ry Belle in;
> When from their Eyes sweet Ruin flies,
>   We die at *Ballyspellin.*   (53–56)

Such fair-sexing was bound to get a reaction from Swift. He replied in the style of the excremental poems, though without their underlying horror:

> Those pocky Drabs
> To cure their Scabs
> You thither are compelling
> Will back be sent
> Worse than they went
> From nasty Ballyspellin[.]   (13–18)

Sheridan was profoundly annoyed at the crudity of Swift's

"Answer."[7] In his friend's opinion, Swift could overstep the limits of raillery too.

Both poets got more pleasure than pain from their poetic rivalry, but they constantly ran the risk of offending each other, and their mutual friends, by neglecting the rules for raillery of the poem "To Mr. Delany." At times, insult predominated over compliment in their teasing, and they both went in for jokes about irredeemable defects—a line of attack Swift had specifically forbidden:

> Reproach not tho in jest, a Friend
> For those Defects he cannot mend;
> His Lineage, Calling, Shape or Sense
> If nam'd with Scorn, gives just Offence.   (67–70)

A long series of poetic jokes about the length of a friend's nose proves that Swift and Sheridan paid only lip-service to this rule. Swift mentions a similar rule for satire in his "Verses on the Death of Dr. Swift," and the likeness of the two precepts proves that raillery and satire were associated in his mind:

> "His Satyr points at no Defect,
> "But what all Mortals may correct;"   (463–64)

In theorizing about both raillery and satire, he seems to assume a moral view of comic art, a view implying that laughter should be directed only at certain, proper objects. Fielding and Dickens shared an extreme variation of this theory, believing that laughter at a "true good Action," in Joseph Andrews' words, was impossible.[8] It caused them an infinite amount of trouble, for instinctively they created their comedy out of whatever materials were handy. They could offer no adequate explanation for the occasional ridiculousness of a Parson Adams or Tom Pinch. Nineteenth-century comic theorists were closer to the truth in postulating that laughter is amoral, and comic artists cannot control its outbreak in themselves or in their readers.

Swift was probably aware that in his day satire was coming under attack, and probably saw that amoral satire was especially vulnerable. Stuart Tave, in *The Amiable Humorist* (Chicago, 1960), has given an account of the progressive antagonism toward satire that gained ground among writers like Addison and Steele. As a man of his time and particularly as a clergyman, Swift accepted the traditional moral view of satire—a view that persists in some circles today. In practice, his comic art veered far from the goal. A. E. Dyson has expressed his puzzlement at Swift's tendency in *Gulliver's Travels* to laugh at matters that never touch upon morality: "The Lilliputians are ridiculous not only because they are immoral, but because they are small. . . . Gulliver himself becomes ridiculous when he is placed beside the Brobdingnagians; whose contempt for him, once again, is not wholly, or even primarily, a moral matter."[9] Dyson should hardly be puzzled, for a completely moral satire is simply not within the reach even of a great comic artist, or *especially* of a great comic artist.

Swift violated his own rules, and with enormous gusto. Not only did he make fun of Dan Jackson's nose, but he mercilessly teased Lady Acheson for her leanness in some of the best poems he wrote for her. In almost all the poems written at Market Hill, Sir Arthur Acheson's seat, the lady appears to accuse Swift of calling her names like "Skinny" and "Snipe." Name-calling was the least of his poetic resources. The jogging meter of "My Lady's Lamentation and Complaint against the Dean" (1728) provides a skillful rhythmic analogue for both the lady's angularity and the abrupt gracelessness of the movement described:

When my elbows he sees
Held up by my knees,
My arms, like two props,
Supporting my chops,
And just as I handle 'em
Moving all like a pendulum;
He trips up my props,
And down my chin drops,   (25–32)

The comparison of the lady to a clock and the reference to her as a "useless machine" (36) imply likewise that her boniness is unnatural and unlovely.

The reduction of a woman to an object and the way style works to accomplish it recall "The Furniture of a Woman's Mind" (1727).

There, by listing rapidly a number of unrelated qualities, Swift breaks a personality into discrete units. His legalistic-auctioneering manner implies that the bits and pieces are both trivial and lifeless. Such a woman, he might say, has no real self at all. Yet "My Lady's Lamentation" is wholly different from "The Furniture of a Woman's Mind." A normally brutal satiric device, in a context touched by raillery, can coexist with affection.

Affectionate or not, this kind of thing might wear away a woman's patience, and the evidence indicates that Swift offended Lady Acheson and her friends just as Sheridan had offended him. In "A Panegyrick on the D—n, in the Person of a Lady in the North" (1730) the lady ironically praises Swift for his accomplishments in various household roles. His role as jester, the lady says, has never yet cost him a friend. He knows precisely how far to go and when to leave off his teasing, and he adjusts his joking delicately to the tastes of the courtly and the crude. Read in reverse, this passage says much about the reception of his raillery, and Faulkner adds a footnote: *"The neighbouring Ladies were no great Understanders of Raillery."*[10]

The ladies may have been no great understanders, but Swift required an inordinate amount of understanding. Lady Acheson showed great good nature in forgiving, and even appreciating, the small imaginative masterpiece "Death and Daphne" (1730). This poem for her starts with a slight joke (the subtitle reads "To an agreeable young Lady, but extremely lean") and spins out an incredible tale that is at once wildly fantastic and realistically detailed. The detail in itself is not surprising: every critic has noticed Swift's use of the concrete. But for the rich play of mind that works the details into an imaginative whole, critics have seldom given him enough credit. By reputation, his poetry lacks "sublimity" and "imagination." In fact, the consistency and integration of detail in poems like "A Description of a City Shower" and "Death and Daphne" rival the manipulation of the concrete in such un-Swiftian poems as "The Eve of St. Agnes."

In "Death and Daphne" Pluto decrees that Death shall take a wife, so that his offspring, following their father's trade, can help populate the underworld. The ghosts of coquettes consult upon his courting dress, and the list of his accouterments is a fine example of Swift's use of imaginative detail:

> From her own Head, *Megæra* takes
> A Perriwig of twisted Snakes;
> Which in the nicest Fashion curl'd,
> Like *Toupets* of this upper World;
> (With Flow'r of Sulphur powder'd well,
> That graceful on his Shoulders fell)
> An Adder of the sable Kind,
> In Line direct, hung down behind.
> The Owl, the Raven, and the Bat,
> Club'd for a Feather to his Hat;
> His Coat, an Us'rer's Velvet Pall,
> Bequeathed to *Pluto,* Corps and all.   (21-32)

The transformation of the otherworldly appurtenances into articles of earthly dress recalls another of Swift's metamorphoses—the change from cottage to church in "Baucis and Philemon." He observes in both poems the same nicety about particulars that makes the metamorphoses engagingly and plausibly complete.

Thus dressed, Death makes his visit to Daphne, who falls instantly in love:

> For, such a Shape of Skin and Bone
> Was never seen, except her own: (61-62)

Thinking to entertain him with her wit, Daphne asks him a series of questions, and here Swift demonstrates his poetic skill in several ways at once: in his use of detail, in his knowledge of female slang, in creating the two overlapping worlds of the eighteenth-century female and Pluto's realm. In fine, funny verse, the lady asks:

> If *Florimel* had found her Love
> For whom she hang'd herself above?
> How oft a Week was kept a Ball
> By *Proserpine,* at *Pluto's* Hall?
> She fancy'd, those *Elysian* Shades
> The sweetest Place for Masquerades:
> How pleasant on the Banks of Styx,
> To troll it in a Coach and Six!   (81-88)

Only the boldest of wits would think of rhyming "Banks of Styx" with "Coach and Six" or conceive of Hades as a "sweet" place for masquerades, or come up with a phrase as delightfully out of place as "troll it."

But Daphne's hopes are dashed. As if by chance Death lays a tentative finger on Daphne's hand and finding it as dry and cold as lead, fearfully runs away. This climax reverses the reader's expectations, for by rights Death's touch should scare the lady: she should feel the "Damp" (97) around her heart. But the final action, though it caps the joke, is less interesting than the imaginative by-play that has gone on earlier. The raillery on the lady's leanness is just an excuse for the poem, the real merit of which lies in the exercise of Swift's facile imagination.

Some of the jokes, though too obvious to be interesting poetically, will raise inevitable questions for the biographical critic. Does Death's deportment as a beau and the lady's as a coquette reveal the author's misunderstandings and prejudices about marriage? In life he interfered between Stella and a suitor and violently opposed his sister's marriage. In poems like "The Progress of Marriage" (1722) and "Phillis, Or, the Progress of Love" (1719), he seems to be uncommonly hard on people who make matrimonial mistakes. Courtship in Swift evokes more ideas of coquetry and foppishness than ideas of love, and "Death and Daphne" takes its place in a long history of satirical Swiftian comments on the process of making a match. Perhaps he was trying to exorcise an inclination to woo the unattainable lady himself by proving how foolish love and marriage were. In that case the frightened "old batchelor" Death is a projection of himself; the jokes about the specter's macabre appearance are a reflection of his knowledge that—at sixty-three—he cut a poor figure as a lover; and his continual gibes at the lady's leanness are an attempt to deny her attractiveness and his attraction by denying her a sexual identity.

"On Cutting down the Old Thorn at Market Hill" (1728) shows that Swift did not restrict his raillery to the lady of the manor, but took on Sir Arthur Acheson as well. The poem has its origin in a quarrel between Sir Arthur and himself over the felling of a sickly and bothersome thorn on the Acheson estate. Sir Arthur might well have been furious at the destruction of the tree and Swift in more than common need to oppose him, for in Ireland

(and in most of Scotland) few acts were more sacrilegious in the popular mind or more likely to bring on continued bad luck than the cutting of a thorn tree. Even if Sir Arthur did not credit the superstition himself, he would have known that from this point on his tenants would feel that his luck was out and so be more inclined to disobey him.[11] With these facts in mind, Swift brings in every literary convention he can think of to make the incident seem blown out of proportion. By subjecting the matter to all sorts of literary ridicule, he hopes to laugh Sir Arthur out of his anger. At the same time, he reveals his familiarity with various literary forms.

The poem is a pastiche of epic, romance, pastoral, and revenge tragedy. Swift adapts all these genres to his own purposes, rather than trying to annihilate them in the manner of the excremental parodies. The effect he achieves is analogous to the mock-heroic in that he satirizes a modern event while sparing, essentially, the artistic forms he uses. The many epithets in the poem are unusual for him, who tended never to waste words in adjective-noun combinations. "Spacious Thorn" (4), "spreading Shade" (7), "fruitful Plain" (10), "dire Event" (32), "pensive Mood" (37), "bloody *Caitiff*" (88)—all derive from poetic traditions and help to raise the cutting down of a tree to an act of heroic proportions. They produce a literary magnification of the event, and the magnification produces in turn a sense of comic melodrama.

The second stanza, in which the village maid hangs garlands from the boughs and sings, secure from satyrs, beneath the spreading shade, evokes the pastoral tradition. The third stanza, in which the valorous knight, Sir Archibald, the "Lord of all the fruitful Plain" (10), comes to listen to the rural songs, combines the pastoral with the epic romance. The fourth stanza deliberately strains the reader's credence with a high-flown "poetic" compliment. Sir Archibald's name will last "for Ages" (14), sung by bards of "highest Fame" (15). The antique diction of the next stanza—"But Time with Iron Teeth I ween" (17)—draws from the poetry of the past to dignify the trivial present and looks forward to the equally out-dated diction in the rest of the poem: " 'Then bloody *Caitiff* think on me' " (88). Nature's response to the cutting of the thorn awakens an echo from the late Renaissance:

> Dame Nature, when she saw the Blow,
>   Astonish'd gave a dreadful Shriek;
> And Mother *Tellus* trembled so
>   She scarce recover'd in a Week.   (25-28)

Compare Milton's lines on the Fall:

> Earth felt the wound, and Nature from her seat
> Sighing through all her Works gave signs of woe,
> That all was lost.[12]

The appearance of the sylvan powers and the omens they send may have several literary sources. Certainly heroic poetry abounds with demigods and with omens of impending doom. The prophecies uttered by the thorn "in a shrill revengeful Tone" (55), the list of punishments in store for each of the accomplices to the crime, show that Swift knew very well what the popular beliefs were. They probably take their form from the prophecies in revenge tragedy. The thorn might be a vegetable incarnation of Margaret in Shakespeare's *Richard III*. Out of a medley of serious poetic traditions, Swift has created a comic gem. For the sources, the poem betrays nothing but appreciation and affection.

Next to "Death and Daphne" and the verses "On Cutting down the Old Thorn," the best of the Market Hill poems is "The Grand Question debated. Whether Hamilton's Bawn should be turned into a Barrack or a Malt-House" (1729). For complex bibliographical reasons, the poem has both an Irish and an English title; and the English title ("A Soldier and a Scholar: Or the Lady's Judgment Upon those two Characters In the Persons of Captain – and D–n S–t") gives the better indication of the basic joke. Swift delighted, somehow, in the notion that Lady Acheson was impatient of his company and preferred the companionship of anyone else. For example, in "Lady A–S–N Weary of the Dean" (1728?) he pictures his friend suggesting to her husband excuses to get rid of their guest:

> Or you may say—my Wife intends,
>   Tho' I should be exceeding proud,
> This Winter to invite some Friends,
>   And Sir I know you hate a Crowd.   (21-24)

This is raillery of a curious kind, for it rallies Swift himself as much as the lady. The same joke underlies "The Grand Question debated" and provides the excuse, again, for the writing of the poem.

The verses open with Sir Arthur suggesting to his wife that Hamilton's Bawn, a large old barn originally used for sheltering cattle, be converted to a malt-house. The knight's reasons are eminently prudent and well thought out, but his wife is not impressed:

> THUS ended the Knight: Thus began his *meek* Wife:
> It *must,* and it *shall* be a *Barrack,* my Life.   (25–26)

The lady complains that they have no company but the unkempt Dean Swift, and a barrack would provide them with a captain who would keep the dean under control.

Lady Acheson loses the argument. But Hannah, her maid, takes up the cause over the dressing-table and, speaking for the lady, argues the virtues of the imaginary captain and the faults of the real Dean Swift. The rest of the poem is Hannah's. The fantasy she spins about the arrival and behavior of the captain rivals in completeness of detail the fantastic plot of "Death and Daphne" and shows, once more, Swift's imaginative scope. But the real merit of the poem lies rather in his conversational expertise. Mrs. Harris and Mary the cook-maid distort the lines of verse in their monologues, and the effect of conversation depends somewhat on this artificial device. Swift conveys Hannah's voice within the limits of the anapestic line. He adapts his chosen verse form to the variations in her tone:

> And now my Dream's out: For I was a-dream'd
> That I saw a huge Rat: O dear, how I scream'd!
> And after, me thought, I had lost my new Shoes;
> And, *Molly,* she said, I should hear some ill News.   (49–52)

Not only do the anapests convey Hannah's tones, but Swift molds the line to fit the speech of the captain, Sir Arthur, and Lady Acheson. These voices come through Hannah in the course of her fantasy, but each has a character of its own, distinct from

Hannah's. In talking to Sir Arthur, the captain assumes an air of courtliness, and the two vie in courtesy:

> Good Morrow, good *Captain,*—I'll wait on you down,—
> You shan't stir a Foot—You'll think me a Clown—
> For all the World, *Captain,* not half an Inch farther—
> You must be obey'd—your Servant, Sir *Arthur*;   (77–80)

In talking to Lady Acheson, the captain is gallant while the lady is demure:

> You're heartily welcome: But as for good Chear,
> You come in the very worst Time of the Year;
> If I had expected so worthy a Guest:—
> Lord! Madam! your Ladyship sure is in jest;   (121–24)

At table, the captain reveals his true nature, as a kind of *miles gloriosus,* in the best of the speeches. He attacks the scholar with a few glancing references to Dean Swift. And after a contemptuous remark about classical authors ("'Your *Noveds,* and *Blutraks,* and *Omurs* and Stuff,'" 159), he launches into a personal history:

> "My School-Master call'd me a Dunce and a Fool,
> "But at Cuffs I was always the Cock of the School;
> "I never cou'd take to my Book for the Blood o'me,
> "And the Puppy confess'd, he expected no Good o'me.
> "He caught me one Morning coquetting his Wife,
> "But he maul'd me, I ne'er was so maul'd in my Life;
> "So, I took to the Road, and what's very odd,
> "The first Man I robb'd was a Parson by G--.
> "Now Madam, you'll think it a strange Thing to say,
> "But, the Sight of a Book makes me sick to this Day."   (163–72)

In the eighteenth century, and until the twentieth, only novelists attempted to render conversation as realistically as Swift. Pope accommodated the human voice in verse, and beautifully, but the voice he imitated was usually his own or a friend's of equal social status. Swift reveled in the imitation of all sorts of voices, even preferring the low-class; and "The Grand Question debated," starting from a bit of raillery, goes on to show his skill in impersonating four completely different people.

As another study in mimicry and another example of raillery involving servants, "To Their Excellencies the Lords Justices of Ireland. The Humble Petition of Frances Harris, Who must Starve, and Die a Maid if it miscarries" (1701) deserves more than passing mention. Its virtues are much the same as those of "Mary the Cook-Maid's Letter." The "Petition" is by far the more successful of the poems, but the difference lies mostly in degree. Swift provides, for the reader's relish, more characters and more colloquialisms and more examples of servant-class sententiousness and "gentility":

> 'Tis not that I value the Money three Skips of a Louse;
> But the Thing I stand upon, is the Credit of the House;   (38–39)

Among Mrs. Harris' friends stands Swift himself, and his portrait as the woman's sweetheart accounts for some of the effectiveness of the poem. He comes across as mercenary, jealous of his status, and comically concerned to distinguish his profession from that of an astrologer. Here (and examples are rare) Swift makes light fun of himself and his sexuality:

> So the *Chaplain* came in; now the Servants say, he is my
>   Sweet-heart,
> Because he's always in my Chamber, and I always take
>   his Part;   (50–51)

Serious self-satire would weigh the poem down. Righteousness would spoil its charm. Swift maintains the buoyancy of the "Petition" by departing from two typical attitudes toward himself and joining in the general mirth. The humanness of everyone in the poem, including Swift, may have helped make it the most frequently anthologized of all his verses.

The charming poem "On the Little House by the Church Yard of Castleknock" (1710) makes a neat contrast to the low-life humor of the "Petition." A major purpose of Swift's here is to parody the Renaissance "house" poem that Pope refurbished for the Augustans. Instead of praising the avenues and apartments of a great man's mansion, Swift makes a series of ridiculous analogies to poke fun at the tiny building that his friend, Archdeacon Walls, used as a vestry. But along the way he brilliantly captures the half-peremptory, half-condescending attitude of "Madam" in lines that prove him as skillful in reproducing upper-class accents as he is in versifying servant speech:

> Pray reach that Thing here to the Child,
> That Thing, I mean, among the Kale,
> And here's to buy a Pot of Ale.   (52–54)

The repeated identification of the vestry as a "Thing" at once ridicules the building and adds to the characterization of "Madam": the object she wants is almost beneath her. The vestry is really for the child, and those who would value it—especially Archdeacon Walls—get their comeuppance in Swift's raillery.

Sometimes raillery is the heart and soul of a Swiftian poem, sometimes merely a way of getting a poem started. Sometimes it consists in small touches of familiarity. In the verses "To Mrs. Biddy Floyd" (1708), for example, Swift uses the prosaic "clay" to describe the main ingredient in the making of the lady, and he ends the poem, deliberately, on the flat and humorous note of her name.

> *Jove* mix'd up all, and his best Clay imploy'd;
> Then call'd the happy Composition, *Floyd*.   (11–12)

Sometimes the raillery is advanced by means of a full-blown portrait, and sometimes it consists of a slight but brilliant character sketch, like this of his old servant in "Dingley, and Brent. A Song" (1724):

> You tell a good jest,
> And please all the rest,
> Comes Dingley, and asks you, What was it?
> And curious to know,
> Away she will go
> To seek an old rag in the closet.   (13–18)

Almost all Swift's social poems are touched by raillery in one way or another. And that is why "Cadenus and Vanessa" (1713) is so curious an exception. Its closest analogue lies not in the Stella poems or in the poems to Lady Acheson, but in the extremely formal verses "To Lord Harley on his Marriage," written just before it. At the writing of the poem, Lord Harley, son of the Earl of Oxford, was not an intimate of Swift's, and the poet always had a tendency to founder (notoriously, in the odes) when faced with a subject he knew very little of. The generalities, the uninspired allusions, could apply equally well to any stranger. Swift compares the younger Harley to Apollo and Endymion, and his bride to Aurora and Diana. The only glint of originality comes with the allusion to Aurora, for Swift probably had in mind the bride's red hair.

With this exception, the poem would be devoid of interest, merely a gesture to please the father of the groom—but the same themes that appear in "Cadenus and Vanessa" have their precedent in the verses "To Lord Harley." Just as Pallas has tutored Vanessa, she has cared for the bride and purified her sight so that she can distinguish Harley from "the dull, the noisy, and the lewd" (48). Just as the virtues of Vanessa make her a failure in love, so Swift fears for the success of the young Harley:

> A spirit so inform'd as yours
> Could never prosper in amours.   (7–8)

And Harley's search for a "virgin of superior mind" (34), who can reward his merit by loving him, parallels Vanessa's search for a lover who can discern her worth.

The two poems are dissimilar in some respects. "To Lord Harley" may be the only poem where Swift consistently uses mythology without a vestige of humor. Lines like

> For, if those antient Tales be true,
> Phoebus was beautiful as you: (25–26)

simply do not appear—thank heaven—in any of Swift's other poems except the odes. In "Cadenus and Vanessa" the legal machinery of the opening and the ending seems to make sly fun of myth, though the mockery is subtle and doesn't quite come off. Swift himself may not have decided whether he wanted to joke or not.

Despite the different attitudes toward myth, the spirit of the two poems is much the same. Throughout the verses "To Lord Harley" and in the beginning, ending, and panegyrical passages of "Cadenus and Vanessa," it is stiff, artificial, and awkward. "Cadenus and Vanessa" does have good moments, but those moments are not Vanessa's. The visiting ladies are brilliantly coy and malicious, surely just come from cards at the house in "Verses on the Death of Dr. Swift" or "The Journal of a Modern Lady" (1729). The fops are brilliantly inconsequential. Miss Betty and her mother form an amusing vignette:

> Miss *Betty,* when she does a Fault,
> Lets fall her Knife, or spills the Salt,
> Will thus be by her Mother chid,
> " 'Tis what *Vanessa* never did."   (242–45)

And Swift is brutally and powerfully honest with himself. On hearing Vanessa's confession of love,

> *Cadenus* felt within him rise
> Shame, Disappointment, Guilt, Surprize.   (624–25)

The admission of shame and guilt is as realistic as anything in Swift. When he comes to write of Vanessa, however, he treats her like a creature out of the verses "To Lord Harley." Whether she is advancing like "*Atalanta's* Star" (306) or reading Montaigne or failing to patch her face properly, he holds her at a distance and never makes her real.

He never succeeded very well at straight panegyric, unmixed with raillery. Why did he attempt it here? He stood in much the same relation to Vanessa as he did to Stella and Lady Acheson: he was friend and tutor to all three of the women. What is different about his attitude toward Vanessa, that he fails to make the praise more credible—and more affectionate—by means of raillery? The likeliest answer is that he was trying deliberately to fend her off. Raillery, with the intimacy it implies, was the wrong technique for his purposes. With Stella and Lady Acheson, who made no demands on him, he was spontaneous and demonstrative in his poetry and letters. With Esther Vanhomrigh, who loved him passionately, he was thoroughly rational and contained. Ehren-preis has noticed in the letters to Vanessa "how hard it would be to decide from the language how well he knew the recipient of the letter or what sort of connection there was between that person and himself . . ."[13] The same analysis would serve for "Cadenus and Vanessa," and perhaps the same reason would account for the distance in both: Swift wanted desperately to transform an explosive relationship into a placid understanding. This answer supports the interpretation of "Cadenus and Vanessa" as an attempt to persuade Vanessa that she is too good for Swift, with the further implication that she should let him alone.

In the poems treated above, raillery has provided an index to the kind of intimacy Swift has wished to convey. From the daring raillery of the poems to Sheridan and Lady Acheson to the subtle familiarity of the lines "To Mrs. Biddy Floyd" to the absence of teasing in "Cadenus and Vanessa," the degree of raillery has indicated the degree of acknowledged affection. In another study one might even turn to raillery in attempting to answer questions about the nature of Swift's relationships.

Raillery serves a different purpose in "An Apology to the Lady C—R—T" (1725) and "Part of the Seventh Epistle of the First Book of Horace Imitated" ("*HARLEY,* the Nation's great Support," 1713). Here Swift foregoes his paternal teasing of others and cultivates another tone entirely—his Horatian voice. He rallies himself, as Horace did, either by implication or through the mouths of others. In both cases, Horace provides the precedent for the technique, even though the "Apology" is not explicitly Horatian. In Swift, as in Horace, the technique flatters by seeming to suppose that the person addressed is better than the writer. It reverses the superior impression that ordinary raillery creates, as the writer assumes the posture of an inferior. Of course, the reader is not to take the posture as literally true, but it does give the compliment a certain twist. Swift's raillery on himself links, again, his social poems to his satirical writings, for the self-satire in *Gulliver's Travels* and many other works resembles the self-mockery in the "Apology" and the imitation of Horace.

"Horace, Epist. I. VII" proceeds along the same self-deprecatory lines as "Horace, Lib.2.Sat.6" ("I often wish'd, that I had clear"), treated in Chapter 1, above. In the former, however, Swift sets up

Harley as an explicit superior—not only in status and power but also in his ability to "crack a Jest" (15). In describing Harley as one who "Loves Mischief better than his Meat" (14), Swift gives him a power he himself usually enjoys and makes him a compliment he himself would value. In contrast to the easy, self-assured maker of jests, Parson Swift appears the humble, harmless butt. The poet even makes light of his literary ambitions, using the same sort of language he would use for a Grub-Street hack:

> Of late indeed the Paper-*Stamp*
> Did very much his Genius cramp;
> And, since he could not spend his Fire,
> He now intended to Retire.   (43–46)

Swift cannot believe that so great a man as Harley would condescend to invite him to dinner. He replies to the invitation coldly, and Harley interprets his coldness as insolence. (Swift enlarges on a favorite Horatian theme: that people mistake his humility for pride.) Meeting Harley a few days after, he "sneaks" to the chariot and offers lame excuses. His part in the conversation is a model of discomfiture; his words, the words of a shy country parson unable to assimilate the friendly gesture of a great man:

> *My Lord—The Honour you design'd—*
> *Extremely proud—but I had din'd—*
> *I'm sure I never shou'd neglect—*
> *No Man alive has more Respect—*   (67–70)

Even after Swift is dean, Harley retains the upper hand, and again superiority lies in skill at raillery. He rallies Swift on his supposed passion for money until the dean bursts out in anger and demands that he stop.

In "Horace, Epist. I. VII," Swift is the butt of both Harley's jokes and his own, and the inversion of his usual position conveys the compliment. In "An Apology to the Lady C—R—T," the lady is too august a figure to make jokes at his expense. He must rely on his own self-deprecation to establish his Horatian voice. As in the imitation, he cannot believe that the lady would invite him to dinner, but he adds a new and effective touch. The messenger is "so trim and nice" (23) and Swift feels so inferior, even to a squire, that he fears his request for a repetition would be rude. Getting ready for dinner presents even greater problems. He brushes his beaver, like a schoolboy eager to make a good impression, and "trudges" (28) into town (the word seems to sum up the impression of a valiant but pitiful little figure). Apparently rebuffed at the door, he returns the next day to make his apology for not waiting. Just as he "sneaks" to the chariot in the Harley poem, he "steals" through the crowd. Just as he apologizes to Harley in broken sentences, so here he falters, hemming and hawing. The lady accepts his apology and promises to visit him.

At this point he momentarily drops his humble manner and assumes his beloved role of gadfly to the great. The voice is still Horatian, for Swift is making a case for simple food and homely entertainment, but his description of the lady's stomach as "clog'd with costly Fare" (105) and his treatment of her fright and fatigue in walking could be placed just as well in a poem to one of his female pupils. From her behavior during the walk, he takes an excuse for his offense and compares her discomfort in the country to his discomfort among courtiers, coxcombs, and the majestic great. This time Swift's raillery upon himself defines his position as a country sage and makes its compliment by explaining his rustic flight from the "living Lusture" (166) of the lady's eyes.

The concept of raillery does not account for the whole appeal of Swift's poems to his friends. Other factors—the richness of his imagination, his facility at reproducing conversation, his skill in sketching a character portrait—help to establish for the social poems an audience wider than the circles they were written for. But these other factors operate in all his poetry, whereas raillery is the distinctive mark of his intimacy and freedom from constraint. For the reader already acquainted with the power and the violence of Swift's hatred for certain people, his intransigence on certain issues, raillery adds a new dimension. It completes the picture of Swift by giving evidence of attributes the critics too often neglect—his playfulness and his tenderness. These attributes, in the form he has shown them, give the poems a universality of appeal even he could not suspect.

8. Poems of Anger

Nothing could make Swift angrier than politics. He had considerable experience in the public life of his day and intense feelings about the major events. The question was whether he could control those feelings well enough to make them amenable to poetry. Judged by the response of his contemporaries, his success is not open to doubt. Harley and Bolingbroke knew what they were doing when they employed him as a political writer from 1710 to 1714. From the first they saw the incendiary appeal of poems like "Sid Hamet's Rod," and early entries in the *Journal* show Swift warming to their praises of his polemic poems. What the Tory ministers wanted was writing with immediate political impact. They evaluated Swift's poems and, later, his *Examiner* papers by the only reasonable standard: his pieces worked. They breathed passion; they reduced well-known enemies to ridiculous caricatures. Now, when the issues are dead, the passions subsided, when the enemies are no longer well known, we may ask how many of the political poems remain accessible and interesting to us.

Works like *A Modest Proposal* and *An Argument against Abolishing Christianity* have won their way through the centuries with accumulated praise. Englishmen who do not contemplate their Irish brethren hungrily and Irishmen who now admit that Swift was probably right can admire the rhetorical ingenuity of

A Modest Proposal and respond to the larger issues of human rights and self-defeating thickheadedness. Southern Baptists, Roman Catholics, and atheists, to name only a few, can overlook Swift's premise in the *Argument* that only Anglicans are Christians and only Christians are good men. They go on to examine the questions of moral and religious authenticity which Swift raises and rejoice in the orotund prose of his persona. In the bulk of his political verse, however, his rhetorical techniques are not especially sophisticated, and his attention is not focused on large issues. The poems did not require breadth and ingenuity to have effect in their time. That is why they are not read by many today, and why I have chosen to omit most of them from this study.

Out of the mass of Swift's political poetry, nonetheless, emerge three of the very best of his poems: "An Epistle to a Lady," "On Poetry: A Rapsody," and "A Character, Panegyric, and Description of the Legion Club" (1736). The first two, dealt with previously in other parts of this book, touch on matters unrelated to politics. "An Epistle to a Lady" is as much a compliment to Lady Acheson and a critique of satire as it is a condemnation of Walpole. The political passages in the verses "On Poetry" follow a long analysis of poetry as a career. Only "The Legion Club" provides a pure example of Swift's ability as a political poet and a true test of whether he could exert sufficient control over his notoriously violent emotions.

Harold Williams seems to think that "The Legion Club" is not a disciplined poem, referring to it as an "uncontrolled outburst."[1] Williams' comments need qualification, for the terrible energy that went into the making of "The Legion Club" is complemented by a remarkable number of rhetorical controls. Swift must have realized that the violence of his opinions was propelling him toward chaos, since he put himself under more stringent restraints than usual and borrowed devices from his prose—devices uncommon in his poetry—to make the verses appear more rational and objective. An inordinate amount of emotion, he must have felt, requires an inordinate amount of control, and the means of regulation he developed make "The Legion Club" possibly the most rhetorical of all his poems.

They do not make it the most controlled of all his poems. Despite the restraints and devices, the poem is always on the verge of becoming an "uncontrolled outburst." The reader feels the strain of Swift's efforts at containing his emotions and perceives that the poem is constantly in danger of erupting into sheer violence. The result is that the reader never quite trusts the poet or believes that he is truly in command. Swift is here master of a rhetorical skill that makes name-calling powerful and gives form to the poem as a whole, but he cannot achieve the kind of skill that leaves a reader nodding in agreement. The audience watches with pleasure, but it only watches.

The question at issue was the attempt of the Irish House of Commons to strip the clergy of some of their tithes—in particular the tithe of pasturage, or "agistment," a sum paid to the vicar or rector by the occupier of pasture lands. Both the Irish and the English courts had decided in favor of the clergy, but the members of the House, many of them landowners, continued to resist. In March 1735/6 the House was presented with a petition against the tithe of agistment, and on the 18th, it gave its opinion. One hundred and ten members voted in support of the graziers who got up the petition, and fifty in support of the clergy. Passed by one house only, the resolution had no force in law, but in fact it was completely effective. Thereafter, tithes were not collected on cattle in Ireland. The vote did not affect Swift's own finances, but he was chary of any threat to the Church and sprang instinctively to its defense. He felt the more strongly because the resolution was so marked a display of the landowners' power and of their contempt both for the Church and for the poor farmers on whom the burden of tithes now fell wholly. "The Legion Club" was his vengeance on the House of Commons.

What the reader will notice first about the poem is the trochaic meter, discussed in relation to "Helter Skelter." Here, as in the other poem, the meter has the effect of rendering the objects of satire mechanical and unnatural. But this poem, unlike the other, capitalizes on the peculiar fascination the meter can evoke of itself. The jogging rhythm creates a comic diversion from the violence of the satire, while the short lines call attention to the odd Butlerian rhymes. These devices point up the artifice, and therefore the discipline, which Swift intended the reader to see.

Throughout the first stanza, the diction and the careful juxtaposition of phrases help convey the impression of an urbane and eminently civilized author in complete control of himself and his subject. The phrase "AS I strole the City" (1) sets the easy, worldly tone. The site of the Parliament House contains both a paradox and a pun, the paradox coming in the nearness of the House to Trinity College and the pun coming in its placement "against" the church:

> Not a Bow-shot from the College,
> Half the Globe from Sense and Knowledge.
> By the prudent Architect
> Plac'd against the Church direct;   (3-6)

The paradox and the pun (attempts at rhetorical control) modify the emotional exaggeration of the phrase "Half the Globe." The succeeding half-told joke with its familiar aside—"you know the rest" (8)—establishes an intimacy between author and reader which Swift will mistakenly take for granted in the later parts of the poem.

Swift follows the careful first stanza with a second that already endangers the reader's trust. It opens with a rhetorical question, the answer to which implies the further progress of the poem:

> TELL us, what this pile contains?
> Many a Head that holds no Brains.
> These Demoniacs let me dub
> With the name of *Legion Club*.   (9-12)

The heads that hold no brains look forward to the image of the madhouse that Swift identifies with Parliament as well as implying that the honorable members are stupid. The word "Demoniacs" and the name "Legion Club" point to his other major metaphor—Hell—while expanding on the first image. In an older tradition, madmen were "demoniac," possessed by evil spirits. And of course, the unclean spirit of Mark 5:9, who answers Jesus with "My name is Legion: for we are many," has taken over the body of a man whom succeeding ages would call mad: "And when he was come out of the ship, immediately there met him out of the tombs a man with an unclean spirit, who had his dwelling among the tombs; and no man could bind him, no, not with chains: because that he had been often bound with fetters and chains, and the chains had been plucked asunder by him, and the fetters broken in pieces: neither could any man tame him. And always, night and day, he was in the mountains, and in the tombs, crying, and cutting himself with stones" (Mark 5:2–5).

Swift compares the House of Commons to the audience at a bearbaiting and the dishonest rabble that gather at the gallows or the pillory. He envisions the honorable members throwing their excrement at a man less guilty than they. Though the image has historical accuracy as a picture of how a mob punished a criminal, it hints again at the image of the madhouse. One of the spectacles that most titillated visitors to an eighteenth-century madhouse was the sight of schizophrenics dabbling in their excrement. It is an image that Swift will develop later in the poem. The rhetorical repetition of the word "such" before each of the comparisons is a slender reed of discipline in the hurricane of this violence. Swift offers no other.

He proceeds by imagining the Devil on the roof-top with his fiery poker pouring cracked stones and molten lead on the "Den of Thieves" (28), the "Harpies Nest" (29), below. The passage reveals an inveterate habit of Swift's: indulging a lust for revenge in print. It leads him to invent for his enemies the most terrifying punishments possible. Thus in "Epistle to a Lady" he imagines the ministers wriggling and howling under the lash of Alecto's whip. In "The Legion Club" he imagines the molten lead scalding the skulls of the parliamentary members. We who are out of touch with the occasion for all this violence and view with tepid objectivity the Parliament's humiliation of the Church of Ireland will find it especially hard to trust the poet's control. He may have hoped that trust would be enforced by the concession to logic at the end of the stanza, where he goes to the trouble of citing authorities—the "Divines" (31) and the gospel—to prove that the Devil is indeed the scourge of God.

What ultimately saves the poem from sheer chaos is not such slight touches as this, but the introduction of two primary metaphors that give the poem artistic shape and a semblance of rational coherence. Though violent in themselves, the metaphors help Swift organize his poem: they permit him to choose his satiric images with consistency and prevent the satire from flying in all directions. The second metaphor—a visit to Hell—begins to take shape in the seventh stanza and those immediately following. It succeeds, but does not displace, the primary image of the madhouse, hinted at in earlier stanzas but fully developed in the fourth, fifth, and sixth. Swift reasons that his own endowment of a school for madmen and fools sets a precedent for the continued existence of the House—as a similar asylum. The picture he gives of the politicians as lunatics resembles so closely his account of Bedlam in "A Digression on Madness" that one might suppose he had the earlier work in mind. The ruthlessness of the satire will produce queer feelings in the modern reader who may think the metaphor ill suited to Swift's purposes. Surely lunatics are not responsible for their actions; yet Swift is pitiless:

> Let them, 'ere they crack a Louse,
> Call for th'Orders of the House;
> Let them with their gosling Quills,
> Scribble senseless Heads of Bills;
> We may, while they strain their Throats,
> Wipe our A[rse]s with their V[otes].   (57–62)

We have three recent studies of eighteenth-century attitudes toward madness to help us understand our unease: Foucault's classic *Histoire de la folie à l'âge classique*, DePorte's *Nightmares and Hobbyhorses: Swift, Sterne, and Augustan Ideas of Madness*, and Byrd's remarkable *Visits to Bedlam: Madness and Literature in the Eighteenth Century*. They show that in creating his metaphor Swift was responding to the idea of madness in a manner typical of his time.

Whom Swift would destroy he first makes mad. His leisurely stroll through a madhouse is a much grimmer version of the cataloguing technique used by Pope in his walk through a portrait gallery ("An Epistle to a Lady"). His development of a gentlemanly persona and his repeated displays of rhetorical control help distinguish him from the lunatics he observes soused in excrement and toasting "Old Glorious" in their urine. Then too, he intends these devices to prove to the reader that he is entertained or amused by the antics, just as visitors to Bedlam on a Sunday afternoon were diverted by the spectacle of insanity.[2] In setting up the cells in stanza four, he calls for a "Hole above for peeping" (46). The variant reading is "to peep in," and we may imagine that he is making the inmates accessible to the kind of spying that Augustan visitors delighted in.

What the Swiftian visitor sees are madmen dabbling in their dung (52), cracking lice (57), and staring, storming, and frowning (55) like mad Jack in *A Tale of a Tub*. He identifies them as animals in a typical Augustan equation of madness and bestiality.[3] Sir Thomas Prendergast is a "rampant Ass" (63) and a "Mole" raising dirt around his cell (73), Richard Tighe and Richard Bettesworth form a "Puppy Pair" (146), John and Robert Allen are again "Asses" (173), and the madmen as a group are "Monkeys" (82), "Brutes" (113), and "Beasts" (225). Byrd quotes from Ned Ward's *London Spy* an instructive combining of the animal and excremental themes: " 'In another Apartment, or *Ward* . . . for the conveniency of drawing a Penny more out of the Pocket of a Spectator, are plac'd the following Animals: First a *Leopard*, who is grown as cunning as a cross Bedlamite that loves not to be look'd at; for as a *Madman* will be apt to salute you with a Bowl of Chamber-lie, so will the *Leopard,* if you come near him, stare in your Face, and Piss upon you.' "[4] Byrd comments, "Here the identification between the lunatic and the worst kind of animalism is automatic and complete . . ."[5] Swift's choice of "antic Shapes" (88) at the entrance to this Hell not only recalls Virgil but capitalizes on another Augustan equation. We might be surprised to find "Poverty" (89) among the shadowy figures, except that the Augustans inevitably associated being mad with being poor and looked upon both states as almost a willful dereliction of middle-class duties.[6]

Swift invents horrific punishments for the inmates, punishments that invoke the satiric lash at the same time that they reflect actual practices in Augustan madhouses:

Tye them Keeper in a Tether,
Let them stare and stink together;
Both are apt to be unruly,
Lash them daily, lash them duly,   (153–56)

Foucault uses as an example of close confinement the discovery of one Godfrey Higgins, who found a concealed door in the asylum of York and behind it a room, not eight feet on a side, which thirteen women occupied by night.[7] DePorte details the brutal "cures" inflicted upon patients, among which beating was in high esteem as a method of "reordering" their minds.[8] But the lashing was more, or rather less, than therapeutic: "To the Augustan mind madness also meant punishment: the madman was punished for being what he was."[9] Disgust did not motivate the punishment so much as fear, springing from the "inescapable conclusion that it is *ourselves* who cause madness, that human beings possess an unpredictable self-altering, self-destructive potential."[10] The madman was a kind of criminal, destructive to himself, negligent about society, and forcing upon his neighbors the kind of fearful truth that made them react with savagery.

We might do well to remember here that madness is a metaphor in "The Legion Club," a way of forcing the outer appearance of the honorable members into a better correspondence with what Swift conceives their inner state to be. The poem is a satire, and the lashing a satiric scourging rather than an actual and brutal beating. But even this reminder does not explain away the hints of sadism in the poem. Satirists have often had to answer to the charge of cruelty, and they have had their answer ready: their satire reforms rather than tortures. Swift foregoes this defense in "The Legion Club" by admitting that his victims are incorrigible:

> Both are apt to be unruly,
> Lash them daily, lash them duly,
> Though 'tis hopeless to reclaim them,
> Scorpion Rods perhaps may tame them.   (155–58)

On the literal level, the inmates may well be "incurables": the eighteenth century was not to hold out hope for recovery from madness until the cure of George III.[11] When we think of the scorpion rods as the satiric lash, however, the image presents some problems. If the objects of satire are not susceptible to reform, then the end of satire—so far as the victims are concerned—is purely punitive, and the punishments proliferate here with such speed and vividness that the reader has every right to suspect Swift of diabolic glee. Swift's cruelty has come under

critical scrutiny in regard to the excremental poems. "An Epistle
to a Lady," with its implications of a nonreformative satire, will
confirm the suspicion. "The Day of Judgement," with its god heed-
less of redemption, will further the argument. And the bulk of the
political poems, with their various engines of torture, will cap the
other evidence. (In "Prometheus, A Poem," 1724, for example,
William Wood is bound with a brass chain and left shivering on the
icy Caucasus, while *"Vultures* eat his growing Liver," 56.) Much
more persuasive than the case for Swift's coprophilia is the case
for his cruelty. By his handling of his material, especially in the
political poems, he raises grave questions about the morality of
satire. When the vengeance is so terrible, the very act of inventing
it inculpates the author. And perhaps, when the vengeance is so
terrible, the very act of imaginative participation inculpates the
reader.

Swift is using the metaphor of madness to distinguish himself
from the honorable members. He may be using the cruelty to distance himself from the metaphor. Like other eighteenth-century
writers (notably, Johnson), he knew that the madness was in himself and he strove to deny it. Byrd, exploring the interrelations
between tragedy and satire, shows that the extraordinary insights
vouchsafed to some madmen approached satiric truths, that Ham-
let and Lear in the Renaissance were satirizing human hypocrisy.[12]
The Augustans largely repudiated this link between the satirist and
the madman, but Swift, in spite of himself, affords a new proof of
the equation. Byrd quotes from the controversial *Letter of Advice
to a Young Poet:* " 'Satyrical Poets* . . . tho' indeed, their Business
is to rake into *Kennels,* and gather up the *Filth* . . . yet I have
observed they too have themselves at the same Time very foul
Cloaths, and like dirty *Persons* leave more *Filth* and *Nastiness,*
than they sweep away.' "[13] We might notice that these "satirical
poets" resemble so closely the "universal reformer" in *A Meditation upon a Broomstick* that we could make a good case for the
authenticity of the first work by referring to the words of the
second: "And yet, with all his Faults, he sets up to be a universal
Reformer and Corrector of Abuses; a Remover of Grievances; rakes
into every Slut's Corner of Nature, bringing hidden Corruptions to
the Light, and raiseth a mighty Dust where there was none before;
sharing deeply all the while in the very same Pollutions he pretends

to sweep away."[14] The point is the same in both works: the satirist, himself mad with righteous indignation, incurs a charge of further folly in thinking that the mad world is worth mending or capable of being mended and in judging that he is the proper person to execute his mission. Swift is suppressing this kind of insight as he writes "The Legion Club." We can tell that his persona, with his debonair movements and speeches, is intended to be entirely free from contaminating fellowship with the madmen. Like "Swift" in "Horace, Epist. I. VII" ("*HARLEY*, the Nation's great Support"), he is supposed to be a "perfect Stranger to the Spleen" (10) and all other modes of derangement. The violence of the man behind the mask may involve a recognition of his kinship with his victims.

But Swift does not forget his rhetorical defenses even in setting up the metaphor of the madhouse. The fifth stanza is punctuated by the phrase "Let them," but the repetition, like the earlier repetition of the word "such," cannot quite give assurance of a careful artistry at work. More useful to him are the comic rhymes in the sixth stanza and the amazing collection of abusive epithets—

At the Parsons, *Tom*, Halloo Boy,
Worthy Offspring of a Shoeboy,
Footman, Traytor, vile Seducer,
Perjur'd Rebel, brib'd Accuser,   (67–70)

They testify at once to Swift's passion and to his rhetorical facility.

His addresses to his muse help define the impression he wants to give. She is "gentle" (79) and "obedient" (75), and, most important, she is Clio, the muse of history. In other poems, the poet has invoked Thalia, the muse of comedy, but here he realizes the necessity of assuming an objective stance. Through Clio he not only claims to be impartial but also warns the Irish politicians of their place in history. And Clio serves a third purpose: to provide another character for the "drama" Swift carefully and consciously sets up to introduce his second major metaphor. He appeals to her to "Shift the Scene" (77), to alter "Time and Place" (78), and with this prelude to the drama he begins the Virgilian account of his descent to the Hell of Irish politics.

The muse stands in the same relation to Swift as the sibyl to

Aeneas, but she acts too as another eye to observe the political scene and confirm Swift's opinion of its horrors. Her presence is the occasion for one of his cleverest comic rhymes:

> Not the Stench of Lake *Avernus,*
> Could have more offended her Nose,   (125–26)

And throughout the Virgilian passage he neglects no opportunity for a show of poetic and rhetorical skill, whether Virgil's or his own. From the imperative "SEE" (81) and "Hark" (82) of the opening lines to the formal apostrophe he takes from Virgil, "ALL ye Gods" (83), he tries to encourage the reader's confidence in his control. The appeal to the muse of history, the creation of a drama, the reliance on the unassailable Virgil, the use of these slight rhetorical tricks—all contribute to the intended impression of an artist, not a madman, behind the scenes.

With the appearance of the Keeper, the two primary metaphors merge. Swift keeps the concept of Hell alive through such lines as

> WHO is that Hell-featur'd Brawler,
> Is it Satan? No, 'tis W[aller].   (137–38)

and "In his Looks are Hell and Murther" (142). But the asylum metaphor is dominant and serves as a frame for the portraits that follow. Among the portraits themselves, one—of Morgan—has qualities atypical of Swift. He presents Morgan as worthy more of pity than of censure, a man blessed with the advantages of a proper education, a deep scholar who took the wrong course and became an ingrate toward his teachers. In a possible allusion to *The Battle of the Books,* Swift pictures Morgan's books coming down from the shelves to punish the ingratitude of their owner. The concessions he makes to Morgan and his pretense to pity recall the strategic mildness of Dryden's portrait of Achitophel. Almost never does Swift mitigate the case against the satiric victim. His resemblance to Dryden here is unprecedented in all his work. It is proof, again, that he was trying to exercise extraordinary caution.

Presented in slightly different terms, Swift's appeal to the painter Hogarth in the penultimate stanza might have countered the impression of self-restraint produced by the preceding stanza

on Morgan. In 1735, a year before the publication of "The Legion
Club," Hogarth had completed his last engraving in *The Rake's
Progress*. It shows Tom Rakewell, having spent his fortune on his
vices, a lunatic confined in Bedlam. His head is shaved according to
the custom of dealing with violent inmates. He is fettered and
forcibly held down, while fellow madmen lie ranting and urinating
on their beds of straw. Swift may have had this scene in mind
when he invoked the name of the painter. Hogarth had well
earned his reputation for the same kind of terrible energy that
characterizes Swift. The poet's request, cast in violent terms, that
Hogarth draw the "Beasts" (225), that he engrave the "odious
Group of Fools" (224), could have run counter to his already
shaky façade of control.

But Swift cultivates a pose for Hogarth just as carefully as he
cultivates his own. Hogarth is not ferocious or ruthlessly irreverent,
but "humorous" (219) and "pleasant" (220), as civilized a gentleman as the poet wants to show himself. Furthermore, Swift reinforces his claim to objectivity by denying that the portraits he has
painted in verse depend upon satiric exaggeration. He tells
Hogarth that he will not need his skills at caricature to depict the
malice and viciousness of the Irish politicians, that he can accomplish the ends of satire through a just likeness. Of course,
these instructions make the satire more incriminating, but Swift
surely has an eye to the protection of his persona.

All the hints noted so far at the nature of his persona would
not by themselves make a full-fledged character, capable of advancing the case for Swift's sanity. But in a few short stanzas
interspersed through the poem, he fleshes out the character. The
persona's gestures in the presence of the Keeper suggest, without
exception, urbanity and easy self-confidence. With a perceptiveness
born of worldly experience, the persona interprets the Keeper's
frown as an invitation for a tip. His explanation for having to
leave—

> But I feel my Spirits spent,
> With the Noise, the Sight, the Scent.   (233-34)

—reveals the tender sensibilities of a gentleman. His taking a pinch
of snuff at the very end of the poem conveys his calmness in the
face of the infernal horrors he has seen.

Swift's civilized pose, though stressing the poet's restraint, serves other purposes as well. All the persona's gestures set him outside the circle of beasts, as a norm and a standard for judging the politicians. Perhaps even more useful to Swift, however, is the way his dramatic role protects him from being conscious of his own anger. If he must work to persuade the reader that he is self-controlled, must he not work also to persuade himself? He fully believed that the trivia of politics should not move him to anger. The lady's refusal to become upset in "An Epistle to a Lady" has all his approval, and his own fury subjects him to self-mockery. "An Epistle to a Lady" gives the reader a glimpse of the torment he felt at the contradiction between his desire to view his enemies as negligible and his real response to them. Like "The Legion Club," it proposes the idea that madness should be entertaining, while half-concealing,. half-confessing the anger that the mad world inspires:

> Safe within my little Wherry,
> All their Madness makes me merry:
>
> .   .   .
>
> (Tho' it must be understood,
> I would hang them if I cou'd:)   (163–64, 169–70)

The alternation between the denial and the acknowledgment of anger proves that Swift could not easily come to terms with the force of his feelings.

Drawing upon "An Epistle to a Lady," one can make solid speculations about the necessity of the role Swift adopts. It stands between him and his anger. In a sense, the role is just a fleshed-out version of the denial of anger in the poem to Lady Acheson. But to the Horatian voice that speaks sporadically in the "Epistle" (and continuously in the social poems), Swift adds a body. He seldom uses such a full-fledged "character" outside his prose. His reliance on it here indicates a need for unusual techniques both to convey an impression of restraint and to enforce control artificially on himself.

Written at the very end of Swift's career, "The Legion Club" is a testament to an old man's fire. Delany thought it excelled all his other poems. That anyone could think so shows how well

Swift has managed his fury. From a writer with feelings less intense, the devices used in "The Legion Club" might make up a masterpiece of artistic discipline, but Swift needed every bit of discipline he could muster, and more, merely to ensure that the reader would not fling the poem away. The façade of "The Legion Club" is like the architecture of New Bedlam in More Fields, the first building in England constructed specifically to house the mad. The splendid neoclassical structure, with perfectly balanced and symmetrical wings, with a graceful formal approach flanked by two mirror-image gardens, housed dark regions of unreason where sane and mad were confounded in common confusion and violence. On the larger scale, New Bedlam was the emblem of the age. On a smaller scale, it was like this poem, formal and rhetorical in its execution, full of underlying hatred and rage and fear.

Like his tender honesty in speaking to women, Swift's anger in poetry had precedents. Perhaps no writer matched him in the cruelty of his effects, for he tended to suppress the humanness of his subjects and then treat them without the mercy that their being human would require. But in the power of his rage he had a rival, the Earl of Rochester, whose own "uncontrolled outbursts" reflected fires just as fierce as Swift's. Even if Rochester did not influence Swift directly, the similarities between the two at least prove that Swift was not alone in his outrage—his fury had a precedent in recent satiric tradition.

At first glance, Swift and Rochester seem worlds apart. What does the notorious Restoration rake have in common with the Dean of St. Patrick's? Words that have a certain bravura charm in Rochester's mouth would be despicable coming from Swift. We would have to overstrain our fancy to imagine Swift uttering the memories and recommendations of Rochester in "The Disabled Debauchee":

> I'll tell of whores attacked, their lords at home;
>> Bawds' quarters beaten up, and fortress won;
> Windows demolished, watches overcome;
>> And handsome ills by my contrivance done.[15]

"A History of Poetry, In a Letter to a Friend" is Swift's punning overview of all verse. He mentions Rochester only to dismiss him:

"Perhaps you WILL-MUTT-er that I have left out the Earl of *Rochester*; but I never was one of his Admirers."[16] This passage is not conclusive proof that he disliked Rochester. The "History" is not meant to be sincere, it is meant only to be funny; and the phrase "I never was one of his Admirers" is very likely an excuse for the pun on "Wilmot." The "History" praises Dorset, Rochester's friend, as an "excellent Poet"—a fact that casts further doubt on Swift's sincerity in dismissing Rochester. Swift may have picked up from the Restoration poet a trick or two about expressing anger.

Swift as a Restoration wit is hardly a ludicrous notion. True, he takes the bawdy element out of the role. Where Rochester might use a sexual image, he uses an excremental one. But in several asexual ways, he approaches Rochester's idea of wit more nearly than Pope, whose overt sexuality seems at first to make him a better match. Rochester defines the man of wit as an enemy of pedants and then, in "Tunbridge Wells" for example, distinguishes himself emphatically from such "stiff" fools. Swift shares this hatred of pedantry. Rochester's "Letter from Artemisia in the Town to Chloe in the Country" shows that he conceives of the wit as an enemy of fops—a view Swift holds too.

Most important, Rochester identifies the wit as a truth-seeker, whose quest often ends in his own unhappiness. The "fine lady" in "Artemisia's Letter" says that this unhappiness is the natural result of inquiring too much:

"When I was married, fools were à *la mode*.
The men of wit were then held *incommode,*
Slow of belief, and fickle in desire,
Who, ere they'll be persuaded, must inquire
As if they came to spy, not to admire.
With searching wisdom, fatal to their ease,
They still find out why what may, should not please,"   (103–09)

These words recall the predicament of Swift's Strephon, whose pursuit of truth in the lady's dressing room was fatal to his ease. Even though Strephon is partly an object of satire, Swift is almost as closely connected to him as Rochester is to his "men of wit." Both poets think of themselves as truth-seekers whose search will lead to despair. The next words of the "fine lady" establish an even stronger link between Swift and Rochester:

> "They little guess, who at our arts are grieved,
> The perfect joy of being well deceived;"   (114-15)

One is tempted to believe that Swift had these lines in mind when he wrote his famous definition of happiness for the hack writer to articulate: *"it is a perpetual Possession of being well Deceived"* (*A Tale of a Tub*, p. 171).

From truth-seeker to truth-teller is a very short step, and one that both Swift and Rochester took. Rochester's definition of wit includes satire as a natural concomitant. But what kind of satire did he wish to write? The evidence shows that, like Swift, he had two typical satiric moods. He seems to have shared with Swift a cerebral belief in the superiority of Horatian satire:

> A jest in scorn points out and hits the thing
> More home than the morosest satyr's sting.
>   ("An Allusion to Horace, the Tenth Satyr of the First Book," 28-29)

On the other hand, the satires show that however much he admired Horace, he owed most of his emotional allegiance to Juvenal. Other poets besides Swift and Rochester have appreciated Horace and written like Juvenal. Dryden and Pope on occasion are prominent examples. But Dryden, at least, seldom rises to the pitch of fury that animates Rochester and makes him Swift's rival in terrible force:

> Bursting with pride, the loathed impostume swells;
> Prick him, he sheds his venom straight, and smells.
>   . . .
> And, with his arm and head, his brain's so weak
> That his starved fancy is compelled to rake
> Among the excrements of others' wit
> To make a stinking meal of what they shit;
> So swine, for nasty meat, to dunghill run,
> And toss their gruntling snouts up when they've done.
>   ("My Lord All-Pride," 1-2, 7-12)

The passage is more imagistic and pictorial than Swift at his usual, but the similarities outweigh the differences. The stark rage recalls the tone of "The Legion Club." The idea of eating excrement is perhaps more violent than any of Swift's variations upon the same theme.

Rochester, like Swift, is frankly coarse and sometimes, though not very often, in the excremental way. He is also irreverent to the point of endangering himself. For a particularly telling libel upon the king, "A Satyr on Charles II," he actually suffered the banishment that Swift only feared. "Impromptu on Charles II," his famous epigram characterizing the king as a breaker of promises, witty in talk and foolish in action, approaches the daring of Swift's political gibes. But most important, Rochester is an angry satirist, as angry as the Swift of "The Legion Club." Whether he gives a graphic description of his reaction to a fool or resorts to outright name-calling, his words have the same wounding energy as Swift's:

> My squeamish stomach I with wine had bribed
> To undertake the dose that was prescribed;
> But turning head, a sudden cursèd view
> That innocent provision overthrew,
> And without drinking, made me purge and spew.
>
> ("Tunbridge Wells," 6–10)

> Crushed by that just contempt his follies bring
> On his crazed head, the vermin fain would sting;
>
> ("On Poet Ninny," 1–2)

In the Juvenalian mode, Swift had a recent model whose violence rivaled his own.

Whether or not the disputed "Farewell" is really by Rochester,[17] the lines have a significance independent of their author. They show that someone's ideal Rochester, Rochester as he must have appeared to many, conceived of his satiric role in much the same way Swift conceived of his. Here is "Rochester" retiring from the fray:

> TIR'D with the noysom Follies of the Age,
> And weary of my Part, I quit the Stage;
> For who in Life's dull Farce a Part would bear,

Where Rogues, Whores, Bawds, all the head Actors are?
Long I with Charitable Malice strove,
Lashing the Court, those Vermin to remove,
But thriving Vice under the rod still grew,
As aged Letchers whipp'd, their Lust renew;
What though my Life hath unsuccessful been,
(For who can this *Augean* Stable clean)
My gen'rous end I will pursue in Death,
And at Mankind rail with my parting breath.[18]

The passage links Swift and Rochester in the contention that satire doesn't do much good, but the most significant link is a matter of tone.

Though the tone of the last line derives ultimately from Juvenal, it has analogues in earlier English satire—in the works, for example, of Hall and Marston. In the Renaissance, critics traced the etymology of "satire" to "satyr" and believed that decorum required poets to write like human satyrs, in a style often crabbed and obscure, always harsh and railing.[19] Hall and Marston followed this formula in creating personae for their verse-satire. When verse-satire was banned in England, Marston and Jonson incorporated satyr-satirists into their plays as characters. Shakespeare continued the tradition with Jacques, Timon, and Thersites. When "Rochester" wrote so fiercely of railing at mankind, he probably had as a conscious precedent the long line of satyr-satirists, characters that were unattractive and incomplete, but generally truthful. When Swift created Gulliver, he was working in the same mode, the tradition of satyr-satire against mankind.[20]

Rochester's most famous universal satire, his "Satyr against Reason and Mankind," raises many of the issues that interested Swift in his satires on man and treats them in a remarkably Swiftian way. The first two lines include Rochester himself in the satire in a way Swift would have appreciated:

Were I (who to my cost already am
One of those strange, prodigious creatures, man)
A spirit free to choose, for my own share,
What case of flesh and blood I pleased to wear,
I'd be a dog, a monkey, or a bear,
Or anything but that vain animal
Who is so proud of being rational.

Even more than Butler, Rochester hits closely Swift's attitude toward reason. Rochester sees that because of reason, man falls into a ludicrous and abhorrent state of pride. The cure? The humiliation that only the satirist can administer. Rochester compares men unfavorably to dogs, monkeys, and bears and eventually finds all nonrational creatures superior.

The fatuous words of the advocate for men who intrudes upon the satire make fun of both the human mind and body, the mind and body that philosophers and scientists extolled from the Restoration through the eighteenth century:

> "Whom his great Maker took such care to make
> That from himself he did the image take
> And this fair frame in shining reason dressed
> To dignify his nature above beast;"   (62–65)

The alternative to prideful reason that Rochester offers is common sense, firmly based upon sense impressions:

> I own right reason, which I would obey:
> That reason which distinguishes by sense
>
> . . .
>
> My reason is my friend, yours is a cheat;
> Hunger calls out, my reason bids me eat;
> Perversely, yours your appetite does mock:
> This asks for food, that answers, "What's o'clock?"   (99–100, 106–09)

In *Gulliver's Travels* and "The Day of Judgement," Swift associates pride with reason. He tries, like Rochester, to cure the fault through humiliation. In *Gulliver* he reverses the conclusions of the old logic-books, which gave the horse as an example of a nonrational and inferior creature,[21] and finds that horses are superior to men. He even ridicules the much praised human body by having the horses comment negatively on Gulliver's shape and positively on their own. The Houyhnhnm master compares man unfavorably to the bestial Yahoos, judging that Yahoos are better because they have no corrupt reason to guide them. In "The Beasts Confession to the Priest, on Observing how most Men mistake their own Talents" (1732), Swift decides that all nonrational animals are superior to man:

Creatures of ev'ry Kind but ours
Well comprehend their nat'ral Powers;
While We, whom *Reason* ought to sway,
Mistake our Talents ev'ry Day:

       . . .

For, here he [Aesop] owns, that now and then
Beasts may *degen'rate* into Men.   (203–06, 219–20)

The alternative, if man can attain it, is common sense.

The question whether a man can achieve virtue bothers both
Swift and Rochester. At the end of "A Satyr against Reason and
Mankind," Rochester speculates about the existence of a single
good man. He does not dare to say that such a man actually exists.
He will say only that if he does exist, "Man differs more from man,
than man from beast" (221). Swift pursues the same question at
the end of *Gulliver*. Pedro de Mendez is a good man, as men go,
but is he truly virtuous? Gulliver seems to think not. Swift leaves
the matter for the critics to dispute.

In their angriest poems, Swift and Rochester have much in
common, but the likeness is, of course, incomplete. Rochester
shows that his grasp of human nature is greater than Swift's,
particularly in regard to motives. Perhaps Rochester is simply
more forgiving than Swift. At least he traces human evil back to
its beginning and makes it more comprehensible. In "Artemisia's
Letter" the "fine lady" recounts the story of Corinna, who begins
a young and much courted beauty and ends a murderess and a
whore. She poisons her lover, a booby squire, after milking him of
all his money. Some of the lines that describe Corinna are
reminiscent of the excremental poems:

"She's a *memento mori* to the rest;
Diseased, decayed, to take up half a crown
Must mortgage her long scarf and manteau gown.
Poor creature! who, unheard of as a fly,
In some dark hole must all the winter lie,
And want and dirt endure a whole half year
That for one month she tawdry may appear."   (202–08)

The words "Poor creature" pinpoint the difference between
Rochester's Corinna and Swift's prostitute nymphs. The disease

and decay that Swift would visit on a whore become, in Rochester, the occasion for genuine pity. Not only does Rochester describe Corinna in pathetic terms, but he also gives the origin of her fall. Apparently, fate decreed that she dote upon a man of wit, who found it dull to love longer than a day, made an ill-natured jest, and left her. The moral of the tale is not that young women should forego fornication and murder, but that Nature kindly provides booby lovers to compensate for witty ones. The ending is not condemnatory, and the reader's reaction is gentler when he knows the cause of the crime. One need only compare the Corinna passage with "The Legion Club" or with the verses "Phillis, Or, the Progress of Love," where Swift shows no pity at all for a pair of foolish lovers, to understand Rochester's greater sensitivity to human motives.

Rochester's interest in the stage may account for another difference between him and Swift. A passage from "Tunbridge Wells" will demonstrate his flair for drama:

> With mouth screwed up, conceited winking eyes,
> And breasts thrust forward, "Lord, sir!" she replies.
> "It is your goodness, and not my deserts,
> Which makes you show this learning, wit, and parts."
> He, puzzled, bites his nail, both to display
> The sparkling ring, and think what next to say,
> And thus breaks forth afresh: "Madam, egad!
> Your luck at cards last night was very bad:"   (98–105)

The description of the lady's mouth, eyes, and breast and the fop's gesture, biting his nail to display his ring, are pictures in motion, probably beyond the powers of Swift. In fact, Swift may not have pictured people at all in the course of writing his angriest poems. If he had, their motives and their gestures would surely have found a place. People became objects to him when he manipulated them in his poetry. Not, to be sure, in real life when they first offended him. In order to goad him to such shocking anger, they must have been fully present to him.

Perceiving their incorrigible vice and folly must have been painful to the reformer in Swift. Perceiving their redeeming humanness must have been painful too, since it would get in the way of judgment. And dealing with his own anger must have been the worst of all. For such a pitch of anger is incredibly painful in itself, as well as being troublesome for the theoretical reasons that confront most satirists—the object of satire is supposed to be trivial, the satirist should be above anger, and so forth. To disguise the pain from his readers and himself, Swift chose the art of poetry.

Afterword

Prose was not exclusively Swift's natural medium. To express the virulent hatred that runs through "The Legion Club" and occasionally threatens to destroy it, he needed poetry as much as any writer ever has. To express the intense friendship he felt for Stella he needed poetry too. His description, to the Reverend James Stopford, of his emotions when Stella lay dying helps to clarify his reasons for turning to poetry: "—Dear Jim, pardon me, I know not what I am saying; but believe me that violent friendship is much more lasting, and as much engaging, as violent love" (*Corr.,* Vol. 3, p. 145). Violence of all sorts was precisely what poetry protected against.

Swift's envy of Houyhnhnm-like aplomb in others (not to mention his envy of the Houyhnhnms) suggests that he placed a very high value on self-control. W. B. Carnochan has noted the evidence in *Lemuel Gulliver's Mirror of Man* (Berkeley, 1968). Swift compliments Bolingbroke for his control of his temper and reveals the misery of his own anger in a letter written in March 1729/30: "I find myself disposed every year, or rather every month, to be more angry and revengeful; and my rage is so ignoble, that it descends even to resent the folly and baseness of the enslaved people among whom I live" (p. 382). He praises Pope for combatting folly and vice "without the least ill effect on your temper" (p. 289). And he admits that he would gladly take on some of Bolingbroke's placidity: "Nothing has convinced me so much that I am of a little subaltern spirit, *inopis atque pusilli animi,* as to reflect how I am forced into the most trifling amusements, to divert the vexation of former thoughts, and present objects.—Why cannot you lend me a shred of your mantle, . . .?" (Vol. 2, p. 334). The phrase "trifling amusements" reminds one immediately of Swift's famous motto, "Vive la bagatelle!" More importantly for us, it recalls his continued insistence that his poems were merely trifles. We may conclude that these "trifles" were paramount in helping him to control himself.

One senses that Swift enjoyed the privacy as well as feared the vehemence of his own emotions. He was too careful and too secretive a man to have exposed them raw. Prose was sufficient to dress out some of his feelings for public appearance, though even in prose he relied heavily on such techniques of indirection as irony, raillery, and the use of personae. They served other purposes besides persuasion. Poetry opened up new possibilities for directing and refining the energy of his feelings. Not all his poems were passionate: a single reason will not account for every bit of verse. What the reason I have given may well account for is the greater range of feeling Swift permitted his poetry to show. To know only his prose is to know him incompletely.

No basic distrust of verse barred him from turning to poetry as an outlet for psychological pressures. He respected poetry itself, though he had reservations about particular kinds of poetry and about professional poets. He and his poet friends must have talked to each other about their work, the merits of other poets, and the threat that lurked in the attics of Grub Street. The evidence indicates that Swift wanted very much to be a good poet himself. To make himself fit for a calling he respected in the abstract and admired in his friends, he must have read with attention the poetry of his predecessors. Among many others, Butler, Rochester, Donne, and Marvell had something to teach him about the practice of his art. What he writ was not all his own—as he ironically admits in "Verses on the Death of Dr. Swift" when he steals that line from Denham. What is surprising is how much *was* his own. The rhetorical strategies he invented ensure that the reader learns what the poet intends to teach, not without pain but always with admiration. They give Swift a basic hold on his audience. The experiments with meter, the imaginative detail, the satiric portraits, the impersonations, the use of classical rhetoric—in these more conventional ways, he pursues his advantage.

His most effective tool, however, is his own forceful personality, shaped by his art. His poetry, technically simple though rhetorically complex, imparts to the reader a sense of contact with an awesomely talented man, whose railing and coaxing cannot be ignored. Not all the poems are great despite Swift's skill at strategies and experiments and impersonations. But Swift was great, and the poems reflect his brilliance.

Bibliography

Aden, John M. "Corinna and the Sterner Muse of Swift," *English Language Notes,* 4 (1966), 23–31.

Ball, F. Elrington. *Swift's Verse: An Essay,* London, 1929.

Butler, Samuel. *Samuel Butler: Hudibras,* ed. John Wilders, Oxford, 1967.

Byrd, Max. *Visits to Bedlam: Madness and Literature in the Eighteenth Century,* Columbia, S.C., 1974.

Carnochan, W. B. *Lemuel Gulliver's Mirror for Man,* Berkeley, 1968.

——"Swift's *Tale*: On Satire, Negation, and the Uses of Irony," *Eighteenth-Century Studies,* 5 (1971), 122–144.

Cotton, Charles. *The Genuine Poetical Works of Charles Cotton, Esq.,* 5th ed. London, 1765.

Crane, R. S. "The Houyhnhnms, the Yahoos, and the History of Ideas," in *Reason and the Imagination: Studies in the History of Ideas 1600–1800,* ed. J. A. Mazzeo (New York, 1962), pp. 231–253.

Davis, Herbert. "Swift's View of Poetry," in *Fair Liberty Was All His Cry: A Tercentenary Tribute to Jonathan Swift 1667–1745,* ed. A. Norman Jeffares (London, 1967), pp. 62–97.

DePorte, Michael V. *Nightmares and Hobbyhorses: Swift, Sterne, and Augustan Ideas of Madness,* San Marino, Calif., 1974.

Donne, John. *The Poems of John Donne,* ed. Herbert Grierson, 2 vols. Oxford, 1912.

Dryden, John. *Dedication of the Æneis,* in *Essays of John Dryden,* ed. W. P. Ker (2 vols., New York, 1961), Vol. 2, pp. 154–240.

——*A Discourse Concerning the Original and Progress of Satire,* in *Essays of John Dryden,* ed. W. P. Ker, Vol. 2, pp. 15–114.

——*The Poems of John Dryden,* ed. James Kinsley, 4 vols. Oxford, 1958.

Dyson, A. E. "Swift: The Metamorphosis of Irony," *Essays and Studies,* new ser. 11 (1958), 53–67.

Ehrenpreis, Irvin. "Letters of Advice to Young Spinsters," in *The Lady of Letters in the Eighteenth Century: Papers Read at a Clark Library Seminar January 18, 1969 by Irvin Ehrenpreis and Robert Halsband* (Los Angeles, Calif., 1969), pp. 3–27.

——*The Personality of Jonathan Swift,* Cambridge, Mass., 1958.

——"Swift's First Poem," *Modern Language Review,* 49 (1954), 210–211.

——*Swift: The Man, His Works, and the Age,* 3 vols. (the last forthcoming), Cambridge, Mass., 1962– .

Ferguson, Oliver W. "The Authorship of 'Apollo's Edict,'" *PMLA,* 70 (1955), 433–440.

Fielding, Henry. *Joseph Andrews,* ed. Martin C. Battestin, Oxford, 1967.

Fischer, John Irwin. "How to Die: *Verses on the Death of Dr. Swift,*" *Review of English Studies,* new ser. 21 (1970), 422–441.

——"The Uses of Virtue: Swift's Last Poem to Stella," in *Essays in Honor of Esmond Linworth Marilla,* ed. Thomas Austin Kirby and William John Olive (Baton Rouge, La., 1970), pp. 201–209.

Foucault, Michel. *Histoire de la folie à l'âge classique,* Librairie Plon, 1961; reprinted Gallimard, 1972.

Greene, Donald. "On Swift's 'Scatological' Poems," *Sewanee Review,* 75 (1967), 672–689.

Horne, C. J. " 'From a Fable form a Truth': A Consideration of the Fable in Swift's Poetry," in *Studies in the Eighteenth Century: Papers Presented at the David Nichol Smith Memorial Seminar, Canberra 1966,* ed. R. F. Brissenden (Canberra, 1968), pp. 193–204.

Huxley, Aldous. "Swift," in *Do What You Will* (New York, 1929), pp. 99–112.

Jack, Ian. *Augustan Satire: Intention and Idiom in English Poetry 1660–1750,* Oxford, 1952.

Jespersen, Otto. "Notes on Metre," *Linguistica,* Copenhagen, 1933; reprinted in *Selected Writings of Otto Jespersen* (London, 1962), pp. 647–672.

Johnson, Maurice. "A Love Song. In the Modern Taste," *Johnsonian News Letter,* 10, No. 1 (1950), 4–5.

——*The Sin of Wit: Jonathan Swift as a Poet,* Syracuse, 1950.

——"Swift's Poetry Reconsidered," in *English Writers of the Eighteenth Century,* ed. John H. Middendorf (New York, 1971), pp. 233–248.

——"Verses on the Death of Dr. Swift," *Notes and Queries,* new ser. 1 (1954), 473–474.

Johnson, Samuel. "Cowley," in *Lives of the English Poets*, ed. George Birkbeck Hill (3 vols. Oxford, 1905), Vol. 1, pp. 1–65.

Kernan, Alvin. *The Cankered Muse: Satire of the English Renaissance*, New Haven, 1959.

Locke, John. *An Essay Concerning Human Understanding*, ed. Alexander Campbell Fraser, 2 vols. Oxford, 1894.

Marvell, Andrew. *The Poems & Letters of Andrew Marvell*, ed. H. M. Margoliouth, 2nd ed. 2 vols., 1930; reprinted Oxford, 1952.

Mayhew, George. "The Early Life and Art of Jonathan Swift," unpublished manuscript.

Milton, John. *John Milton: Complete Poems and Major Prose*, ed. Merritt Y. Hughes, New York, 1957.

Murry, John Middleton. *Jonathan Swift: A Critical Biography*, London, 1954.

O'Hehir, Brendan. "Meaning of Swift's 'Description of a City Shower,'" *ELH*, 27 (1960), 194–207.

Oldham, John. *Poems of John Oldham*, intro. Bonamy Dobrée, London, 1960.

Peake, Charles. "Swift's 'Satirical Elegy on a Late Famous General,'" *Review of English Literature*, 3 (1962), 80–89.

Pope, Alexander. *Epistles to Several Persons (Moral Essays)*, ed. F. W. Bateson, Twickenham Edition (11 vols. London and New Haven, 1939–69), Vol. 3, Part ii (1961).

——*The Rape of the Lock and Other Poems*, ed. Geoffrey Tillotson, Twickenham Edition, Vol. 2 (1940).

Prior, Matthew. *The Literary Works of Matthew Prior*, ed. H. Bunker Wright and Monroe K. Spears, 2 vols. Oxford, 1959.

Quintana, Ricardo. "A Modest Appraisal: Swift Scholarship and Criticism, 1945–65," in *Fair Liberty Was All His Cry: A Tercentenary Tribute to Jonathan Swift 1667–1745*, ed. A. Norman Jeffares (London, 1967), pp. 342–355.

Rochester, John Wilmot, Earl of. *The Complete Poems of John Wilmot, Earl of Rochester*, ed. David M. Vieth, New Haven, 1968.

——*Poems by John Wilmot, Earl of Rochester*, ed. Vivian de Sola Pinto, 2nd ed. revised Cambridge, Mass., 1964.

Savage, Roger. "Swift's Fallen City: A Description of the Morning," in *The World of Jonathan Swift: Essays for the Tercentenary*, ed. Brian Vickers (Oxford, 1968), pp. 171–194.

Schakel, Peter J. "The Politics of Opposition in 'Verses on the Death of Dr. Swift,'" *Modern Language Quarterly*, 35 (1974), 246–256.

——"Swift's 'dapper Clerk' and the Matrix of Allusions in 'Cadenus and Vanessa,'" *Criticism*, 17 (1975), 246–261.

Scouten, Arthur H. and Robert D. Hume, "Pope and Swift: Text and Interpretation of Swift's Verses on His Death," *Philological Quarterly,* 52 (1973), 205–231.

Sedley, Sir Charles. "Song" (1672), in *Restoration Literature: Poetry and Prose,* ed. Cecil A. Moore (New York, 1934), p. 378.

Shakespeare, William. *The Sonnets,* in *The Works of Shakespeare,* ed. John Dover Wilson, Cambridge, England, 1966.

Slepian, Barry. "The Ironic Intention of Swift's Verses on His Own Death," *Review of English Studies,* new ser. 14 (1963), 249–256.

Steele, Richard. *The Tatler,* in *The British Essayists,* ed. Alexander Chalmers, 5 vols. New York, 1809.

Swift, Jonathan. *The Correspondence of Jonathan Swift,* ed. Harold Williams, 5 vols. Oxford, 1963–65.

——*Journal to Stella,* ed. Harold Williams, 2 vols. Oxford, 1948.

——*The Poems of Jonathan Swift,* ed. Harold Williams, 2nd ed. 3 vols. Oxford, 1958.

——*The Prose Works of Jonathan Swift,* ed. Herbert Davis, 14 vols. Oxford, 1939–68.

——*Swift: Poetical Works,* ed. Herbert Davis, London, 1967.

——*A Tale of a Tub: To which is added The Battle of the Books and the Mechanical Operation of the Spirit,* ed. A. C. Guthkelch and David Nichol Smith, 2nd ed. Oxford, 1958.

Tave, Stuart. *The Amiable Humorist,* Chicago, 1960.

Thackeray, William. *The English Humourists of the Eighteenth Century,* ed. William Lyon Phelps, New York, 1900.

Trickett, Rachel. *The Honest Muse: A Study in Augustan Verse,* Oxford, 1967.

Waingrow, Marshall. *"Verses on the Death of Dr. Swift,"* Studies in English Literature, 5 (1965), 513–518.

Ward, Edward. *The London Spy,* 1698-1709; reprinted London, 1964.

Watkins, W. B. C. *Perilous Balance: The Tragic Genius of Swift, Johnson, & Sterne,* Princeton, 1939; reprinted for Walker-deBerry, Inc., Cambridge, England, 1960.

Watt, Ian. "The Ironic Tradition in Augustan Prose from Swift to Johnson," in *Restoration & Augustan Prose: Papers Delivered by James R. Sutherland and Ian Watt at the Third Clark Library Seminar, 14 July 1956* (Los Angeles, Calif., 1956), pp. 19-46.

Webster, C. M. "*Hudibras* and Swift," *Modern Language Notes,* 47 (1932), 245-246.

Williams, Harold. *Dean Swift's Library,* Cambridge, England, 1932.

Notes

1. Reading Swift's Poems

1. Vol. 3, Part ii, of the Twickenham edition, Alexander Pope, *Epistles to Several Persons (Moral Essays)*, ed. F. W. Bateson, 2nd ed. (London and New Haven, 1961), p. 70.

2. *The Poems of Jonathan Swift,* ed. Harold Williams, 2nd ed. (Oxford, 1958), Vol. 2, pp. 735–736. Cited below as *Poems.* I have taken all quotations of Swift's poetry from Williams' edition. Line references are enclosed in parentheses within the text.

3. Vol. 2 of the Twickenham edition, *The Rape of the Lock and Other Poems,* ed. Geoffrey Tillotson (London and New Haven, 1940), p. 177.

4. *The Sin of Wit: Jonathan Swift as a Poet* (Syracuse, 1950), p. 46.

5. "Swift's Fallen City: A Description of the Morning," in *The World of Jonathan Swift: Essays for the Tercentary,* ed. Brian Vickers (Oxford, 1968), p. 180.

6. Ibid., p. 185.

7. "Swift's Poetry Reconsidered," in *English Writers of the Eighteenth Century,* ed. John H. Middendorf (New York, 1971), p. 239.

8. Printing from *Poems,* 1735 (uncanceled state), Davis thus supplies the missing words in line 1. See *Poetical Works,* ed. Herbert Davis (London, 1967), p. 147.

9. See Murry's *Jonathan Swift: A Critical Biography* (London, 1954), pp. 457–459.

10. "Verses on the Death of Dr. Swift," *Notes and Queries,* new ser. 1 (1954), 473–474.

11. "The Ironic Intention of Swift's Verses on His Own Death," *Review of English Studies,* new ser. 14 (1963), 249–256.

12. "*Verses on the Death of Dr. Swift,*" *Studies in English Literature,* 5 (1965), 513–518.

13. "Pope and Swift: Text and Interpretation of Swift's Verses on His Death," *Philological Quarterly,* 52 (1973), 205–231.

14. See "Blue-skin's Ballad." Herbert Davis includes it in the *Poetical Works* as a poem attributed to Swift. The date he gives is 1724–5. Williams argues in *Poems,* Vol. 3, p. 1113, for "some probability" in favor of Swift's authorship. The lines quoted from the "Epistle" are added by Faulkner and later editors after line 192.

15. *A Discourse Concerning the Original and Progress of Satire,* in *Essays of John Dryden,* ed. W. P. Ker (New York, 1961), Vol. 2, pp. 78–99.

16. *A Tale of a Tub: To which is added The Battle of the Books and the Mechanical Operation of the Spirit,* ed. A. C. Guthkelch and David Nichol Smith, 2nd ed. (Oxford, 1958), p. 215. Textual references are to this edition.

17. *Perilous Balance: The Tragic Genius of Swift, Johnson, & Sterne* (Princeton, 1939), reprinted for Walker-deBerry, Inc. (Cambridge, England, 1960), p. 6.

18. "Notes on Metre," *Linguistica* (Copenhagen, 1933), reprinted in *Selected Writings of Otto Jespersen* (London, 1962), p. 666.

19. Janet Barbour suggested this line of argument to me.

20. For the allusion to Butler in "Baucis and Philemon," see C. M. Webster, "*Hudibras* and Swift," *Modern Language Notes,* 47 (1932), 246. For the allusion in "Epistle to a Lady," see note to lines 95–96 in *Poems,* Vol. 2, p. 632.

21. *Samuel Butler: Hudibras,* ed. John Wilders (Oxford, 1967), p. 231. I have taken all quotations of Butler's poem from Wilders' edition.

22. *Augustan Satire: Intention and Idiom in English Poetry 1660–1750* (Oxford, 1952), p. 31.

23. *Swift: The Man, His Works, and the Age* (Cambridge, Mass., 1962–), Vol. 2, p. 26.

24. Harold Williams, *Dean Swift's Library* (Cambridge, England, 1932), pp. 54–55, 74–77.

25. *The Correspondence of Jonathan Swift,* ed. Harold Williams (Oxford, 1963–65), Vol. 4, p. 53. Cited in the text as *Corr.*

26. The citation from Cotton's poem is to *The Genuine Poetical Works of Charles Cotton, Esq.,* 5th ed. (London, 1765), p. 5.

27. Oldham's lines are quoted from *Poems of John Oldham,* intro. Bonamy Dobrée (London, 1960), p. 103.

2. Poems on Poetry

1. See Oliver W. Ferguson, "The Authorship of 'Apollo's Edict,'" *PMLA*, 70 (1955), 433–440.

2. "A Love Song. In the Modern Taste," *Johnsonian News Letter*, 10, No. 1 (1950), 4–5.

3. Herbert Davis, "Swift's View of Poetry," in *Fair Liberty Was All His Cry: A Tercentenary Tribute to Jonathan Swift 1667–1745*, ed. A. Norman Jeffares (London, 1967), p. 65.

4. *Journal to Stella*, ed. Harold Williams (Oxford, 1948), Vol. 1, p. 62. Cited in the text as *Journal*.

3. The Odes

1. "Cowley," in *Lives of the English Poets*, ed. George Birkbeck Hill (Oxford, 1905), Vol. 1, p. 48.

2. Ibid.

3. Quoted in *Poetical Works*, ed. Davis, p. xxix.

4. See *The Prose Works of Jonathan Swift*, ed. Herbert Davis (Oxford, 1939–68), Vol. 2, p. 114.

5. *Swift: The Man, His Works, and the Age*, Vol. 1, pp. 113 and n. 3, 118, 136 n. 1.

6. Ibid., p. 129 nn. 3, 4.

7. Dryden's poetry is quoted from *The Poems of John Dryden*, ed. James Kinsley (Oxford, 1958), Vol. 1, p. 218.

8. See the unpublished manuscript by George Mayhew, "The Early Life and Art of Jonathan Swift," chap. 5, pp. 21–25.

9. *Swift: The Man, His Works, and the Age*, Vol. 1, pp. 116, 138.

10. Ehrenpreis makes this point in "Swift's First Poem," *Modern Language Review*, 49 (1954), 211.

11. Mayhew, chap. 6, p. 35.

4. The Two "Descriptions"

1. *The Tatler*, 9 (April 30, 1709), in *The British Essayists*, ed. Alexander Chalmers (New York, 1809), Vol. 1, p. 147.

2. Ibid.

3. Ibid., pp. 147–148.

4. Ibid.

5. *The Tatler*, 238 (October 17, 1710), in *The British Essayists*, Vol. 5, p. 136.

6. Ibid.

7. For another opinion see Brendan O'Hehir, "Meaning of Swift's 'Description of a City Shower,'" *ELH,* 27 (1960), 194–207.

8. "Swift's *Tale:* On Satire, Negation, and the Uses of Irony," *Eighteenth-Century Studies,* 5 (1971), 134–135.

9. *The Prose Works of Jonathan Swift,* ed. Davis, Vol. 9, 65.

10. Ibid., Vol. 11, p. 137.

11. Ibid., p. 275.

12. Ibid., p. 235.

13. Ibid., p. 273.

14. Ibid., pp. 185–186.

5. The Stella Poems

1. In *Restoration Literature: Poetry and Prose,* ed. Cecil A. Moore (New York, 1934), p. 378.

2. From the series *The Works of Shakespeare, The Sonnets,* ed. John Dover Wilson (Cambridge, England, 1966), p. 67.

3. *The English Humourists of the Eighteenth Century,* ed. William Lyon Phelps (New York, 1900), pp. 39–50.

4. I owe this phrase to the late Reuben Brower.

5. *The Poems of John Donne,* ed. Herbert Grierson (Oxford, 1912), Vol. 1, p. 37. I have taken all quotations of Donne's poetry from the Grierson edition.

6. I thank Neil Rudenstine and Heather Ousby for helpful information about Donne.

7. *The Poems & Letters of Andrew Marvell,* ed. H. M. Margoliouth, 2nd ed. (1930; reprinted Oxford, 1952), Vol. 1, p. 27. Marvell's poetry is quoted from this edition.

8. *The Literary Works of Matthew Prior,* ed. H. Bunker Wright and Monroe K. Spears (Oxford, 1959), Vol. 1, p. 451.

9. *Dedication of the Æneis,* in *Essays of John Dryden,* ed. W. P. Ker (New York, 1961), Vol. 2, p. 227.

6. The Excremental Poems

1. I use the term "excremental" for five poems: "The Progress of Beauty," "A Beautiful Young Nymph Going to Bed," "Cassinus and Peter," "Strephon and Chloe," and "The Lady's Dressing Room." I have chosen the term as a convenient, well known, and fairly appropriate label, even though two of the

poems do not mention excrement and even though a few poems outside the group contain jokes about excretion.

2. See Huxley's "Swift," in *Do What You Will* (New York, 1929), pp. 99–112, and Murry's *Jonathan Swift: A Critical Biography* (London, 1954), pp. 432–448.

3. "Swift's View of Poetry," in *Fair Liberty Was All His Cry: A Tercentenary Tribute to Jonathan Swift 1667–1745*, ed. Norman Jeffares, p. 92.

4. *The Personality of Jonathan Swift* (Cambridge, Mass., 1958), p. 38.

5. Ehrenpreis makes this point in *The Personality*, p. 41.

6. "Corinna and the Sterner Muse of Swift," *English Language Notes*, 4 (1966), 28.

7. Ibid., pp. 30–31.

8. Ibid., p. 27.

9. Donne's lines are quoted from *The Poems of John Donne*, ed. Herbert Grierson (Oxford, 1912), Vol. 1, p. 120.

10. *The Prose Works of Jonathan Swift*, ed. Davis, Vol. 1, p. 240.

11. "On Swift's 'Scatological' Poems," *Sewanee Review*, 75 (1967), 683–684.

12. W. B. Carnochan explains these curious lines as an allusion to Locke's theories of association (*Lemuel Gulliver's Mirror for Man*, Berkeley, 1968, p. 132):

> Ideas that in themselves are not all of kin, come to be so united in some men's minds, that it is very hard to separate them; they always keep in company, and the one no sooner at any time comes into the understanding, but its associate appears with it;

An Essay Concerning Human Understanding, ed. Alexander Campbell Fraser (Oxford, 1894), Vol. 1, p. 529.

13. The italics are mine.

14. I came to these conclusions about men's and women's responses in teaching the poems to a mixed group.

7. The Poems of Daily Social Life

1. Ian Watt identifies the fallacy as the inversion of the fallacy of class. See "The Ironic Tradition in Augustan Prose from Swift to Johnson," in *Restoration & Augustan Prose: Papers Delivered by James R. Sutherland and Ian Watt at the Third Clark Library Seminar, 14 July 1956* (Los Angeles, Calif., 1956), p. 34.

2. *The Prose Works of Jonathan Swift*, ed. Davis, Vol. 5, p. 222.

3. Sheridan is quoted from Volume 3 of *Poems*.

4. Quoted in *Poems,* Vol. 3, p. 968.

5. Ibid., p. 970.

6. Ibid., p. 980.

7. See *The History of the Second Solomon,* in *Prose Works,* Vol. 5, p. 225.

8. Henry Fielding, *Joseph Andrews,* ed. Martin C. Battestin (Oxford, 1967), p. 234.

9. "Swift: The Metamorphosis of Irony," *Essays and Studies,* new ser. 11 (1958), 58.

10. Quoted in *Poems,* Vol. 3, p. 890, note to line 120.

11. I thank John Kelleher for this information about Celtic folklore.

12. Milton's poetry is quoted from *John Milton: Complete Poems and Major Prose,* ed. Merritt Y. Hughes (New York, 1957), p. 396.

13. "Letters of Advice to Young Spinsters," in *The Lady of Letters in the Eighteenth Century: Papers Read at a Clark Library Seminar January 18, 1969 by Irvin Ehrenpreis and Robert Halsband* (Los Angeles, Calif., 1969), p. 15.

8. Poems of Anger

1. *Poems,* Vol. 1, p. xvi.

2. Max Byrd, *Visits to Bedlam: Madness and Literature in the Eighteenth Century* (Columbia, S.C., 1974), p. 39.

3. Michel Foucault, *Histoire de la folie à l'âge classique* (Librairie Plon, 1961; reprinted Gallimard, 1972), pp. 163–170.

4. Edward Ward, *The London Spy* (1698–1709, reprinted London, 1964), p. 311. Quoted in Byrd, p. 45.

5. Byrd, p. 45.

6. Ibid., pp. 22–30.

7. Foucault, p. 164.

8. Michael V. DePorte, *Nightmares and Hobbyhorses: Swift, Sterne, and Augustan Ideas of Madness* (San Marino, Calif., 1974), p. 5.

9. Byrd, p. 54.

10. Ibid.

11. Ibid., pp. 133–135.

12. Ibid., p. 5.

13. *The Prose Works of Jonathan Swift,* ed. Davis, Vol. 9, p. 342. Quoted in Byrd, p. 77.

14. Ibid., Vol. 1, p. 240.

15. *The Complete Poems of John Wilmot, Earl of Rochester,* ed. David M. Vieth (New Haven, 1968), p. 117. Unless indicated otherwise in a note, Rochester's poetry is quoted from this edition.

16. *Prose Works,* Vol. 4, p. 274.

17. See *Poems by John Wilmot, Earl of Rochester,* ed. Vivian de Sola Pinto (2nd ed., rev., Cambridge, Mass., 1964), p. 231, for an argument that lines 1–12 are by Rochester.

18. Quoted from Pinto's edition, p. 150.

19. For a discussion of this subject, see Alvin Kernan, *The Cankered Muse: Satire of the English Renaissance* (New Haven, 1959), pp. 54–63.

20. Though "satyr-satire" was a distinct Renaissance phenomenon and "satire against mankind" was a definite minor genre in the late seventeenth century, I am assuming connections between the two, connections that reached their fullest expression in Swift.

21. See R. S. Crane, "The Houyhnhnms, the Yahoos, and the History of Ideas," in *Reason and the Imagination: Studies in the History of Ideas, 1600–1800,* ed. J. A. Mazzeo (New York, 1962), pp. 231–253.

Index